SNIFFER DOGS

SNIFFER DOGS

How Dogs (and Their Noses) Save the World

by NANCY F. CASTALDO

Houghton Mifflin Harcourt
Boston New York

*For the dogs who work to make our lives better
and the people who love them.*

www.hmhco.com

The text of this book is set in Albertina and Zemestro.
Photo credits can be found on page 153.
Book design by Rachel Newborn

The Library of Congress has cataloged the hardcover edition as follows:
Castaldo, Nancy F. (Nancy Fusco), 1962–, author.
Sniffer dogs : how dogs (and their noses) save the world /
Nancy F. Castaldo.
pages cm
Summary: "Readers will discover how detection dogs are able to use
their noses to find everything from people, both alive and dead, to
explosives to . . . whale poop. These working dogs work to please,
work to play, and work for love." —Provided by publisher.
Audience: 10 and up.
Audience: Grades 4 to 6.
1. Detector dogs—Juvenile literature. 2. Search dogs—Juvenile
literature. 3. Dogs—Sense organs—Juvenile literature. 4. Smell—
Juvenile literature. I. Title.
HV8025.C37   2014
636.7088'6—dc23
2013017612

ISBN: 978-0-544-08893-1 hardcover
ISBN: 978-0-544-93259-3 paperback

Manufactured in China
SCP 10 9 8 7 6 5 4 3 2 1
4500650832

CONTENTS

To see a working dog.
To see the beauty and grace
and agility that they have,
it makes my heart sing.

—Wilma Melville,
founder, National Disaster
Search Dog Foundation

BEST FRIENDS AND HEROES

Eli, a four-year-old bomb-sniffing black Labrador, was assigned to work alongside Marine Pfc. Colton Rusk, an improvised explosive device detection dog handler. The two left for a tour in Afghanistan on September 23, 2010, Colton's twentieth birthday, and became inseparable. In fact, Colton often broke protocol by letting Eli sleep with him on his cot instead of in the regulation kennel on the floor. And on his Facebook page Colton wrote under a photo of Eli, "What's mine is also his." There was no question of the bond the two shared.

On December 6, 2010, just a few months after arriving in Afghanistan, Colton was hit by sniper fire while on patrol and was killed. His dog, Eli, stood guard, crawling on top of his partner's body, not leaving its side, even when Colton's fellow soldiers came to retrieve it.

Colton's family knew how close the two had been. Phone calls home always included news about Eli. When the family

← Colton's mom, Kathy Rusk, wears the photo of her son and his beloved explosive detection dog, Eli.

lost Colton, they decided that Eli needed to come home to them. Thanks to new legislation, the Rusk family was able to petition the military to receive the retired military canine. On February 3, the Rusk family headed to Lackland Air Force Base in Texas to bring Eli home. Eli was formally retired from the military and adopted into the Rusks' civilian home. When Colton's obituary was written, Eli was listed first among his surviving family members.

The sun was shining and a cool breeze blew on the South Indian Pondicherry shore in December of 2004. No one had a clue that a huge earthquake, measuring over 9 on the Richter scale, had shifted the plates underneath the ocean floor more than fifteen miles (25 kilometers) away. A woman named Sangeeta walked on the beach with her three sons and their scraggly yellow puppy named Selvakumar, as she did every day. Her husband had just returned from fishing when he heard the ocean's strange rumblings. Then he saw the waves, close to thirty-three feet (10 meters) high. He ran to a nearby roof and shouted to his wife to run.

She grabbed the hands of her two youngest boys. Her older son, Dinakaran, could run by himself. But when she reached safety, Dinakaran was not behind her. He had run to the family hut only forty yards (37 meters) from the shore. Luckily Selvakumar went after him. The dog clenched the boy's shirt collar between his teeth and coaxed him out of the collapsing hut to safety.

The tsunami that hit the beach that day took thousands of lives across South Asia, but Dinakaran was not among them. Salvakumar was a hero.

There are many stories like these, but your dog doesn't have to save your life or do anything extraordinary for you to know that you share a strong bond. It's easy to see. Just walk in the door and experience a dog greeting: tail wags, tongue licks, and unbridled enthusiasm, just because you came back home. It's what dogs do. They display this behavior in the wild with their puppies, and they act the same with us.

The bond is reciprocated. Dog owners have been known to risk their own lives for their beloved pets. Take Ann Elizabeth Isham, for example. Isham was a first-class passenger on the *Titanic,* one of only four female first-class passengers who perished in the disaster. It is commonly believed that when her Great Dane was denied a place in a lifeboat, she refused to leave without it. Their bodies were both found floating in the sea after the ship sank. Reports say that her frozen arms were wrapped around the dog's neck, but it has never been proven that the woman found floating alongside the dog was actually Ann Isham.

Fortunately, not all the dogs aboard the ship perished. Three tiny dogs were smuggled into the lifeboats by their owners. If Isham's Great Dane had been small enough, without a doubt she would have been one of those owners.

Dogs have been man's (and woman's!) best friend for thousands of years. Scientists aren't quite sure just when dogs, which are descended from wild wolves, became domesticated, but there is plenty of evidence of our early bonding, including ancient burial sites. Archaeologists uncovered evidence of one of the earliest domesticated dogs in a 14,000-year-old joint burial site in Germany, known as Bonn-Oberkassel, which contained the remains of a human and a dog.

Was that dog a pet? Did it help that human hunt? Did they die together? We might never know all the answers, but we can surmise that the dog buried beside the human was important to the person who died. Visitors to fourth-century Roman catacombs can see images of dogs carved into the marble grave markers of their masters.

There are more than seventy-eight million dogs sharing their lives with us in the United States. Dog owners spend on average $1,500 per year on food, treats, boarding, and grooming for their beloved pets. But the people of the United States aren't alone in their enthusiasm for these loyal, furry friends. There are many millions more throughout the world. In fact, dogs are the only animals that have found their way into every human culture.

Captain Kerry W. Foster from Shreveport, Louisiana, and the search and rescue dog Ranger search for human remains in this house destroyed by Hurricane Katrina. All homes being demolished in the Ninth Ward were searched so that no victims were left behind. →

Perhaps the oldest job dogs have had is to help us hunt for food. The artist George Catlin witnessed the relationship between the Native Amer-

In recent years, when Hurricane Katrina devastated Mississippi and Louisiana, many pet owners, like Ann Isham, refused to evacuate and leave their pets; sometimes the worst happened to them, too. Still others were forced to leave their pets behind without any care, because there weren't any provisions made to evacuate these animals. This resulted in the suffering of tens of thousands of pets and the emotional trauma of their owners. The "silver lining" in that tragedy is that Congress passed the Pets Evacuation and Transportation Act in 2006. It requires that all states receiving money from the Federal Emergency Management Agency (FEMA) have a pet evacuation plan in place. The act also grants FEMA the authority to give assistance to people with pets and service animals. FEMA can help with the rescue and care of these animals during and after a disaster.

ican tribes he visited in the 1800s and their dogs. The dogs hunted with their humans and, Catlin wrote, were "equal partners in the chase." He also wrote that "the dog, amongst all Indian tribes is more esteemed and more valued than amongst any part of the civilized world." Even then the dog was used as a symbol of fidelity. Catlin's work is just more evidence of our strong bond and early reliance on working dogs.

George Catlin's *Two Comanche Girls 1834* depicts the wigwam of the Comanche chief, his children, and his dogs. ↓

↑ The days of horse-drawn carriages are over, but many Dalmatians are still being used to guard firefighting equipment and serve as firehouse mascots.

Have you ever seen a spotted Dalmatian at a firehouse? Dalmatians, the famous black and white firehouse mascots, were once indispensable working dogs to firefighters. Once known as the English coach dogs or the carriage dogs, Dalmatians ran alongside horse-drawn coaches, carriages, or steam engines. The smooth-coated, spotted dogs developed strong ties with the horses pulling carriages as early as the seventeenth century. They helped the horses keep pace and protected them from the wild dogs that nipped at their legs. Once at the scene of a blazing fire, the dogs would stand guard, protecting the strong, valuable horses and expensive equipment from thieves while the firefighters fought the flames.

Cheyenne, a therapy dog, is serving in a different way. She visits retired firefighters at the FASNY Firemen's Home in Hudson, New York.

During World War I and World War II, dogs were used to help locate injured soldiers on or near the battlefield. These dogs were often called casualty or ambulance dogs. They also were used by the military as scouts, trackers, sentries, and messengers. In addition, they helped detect mines.

In 1929 dogs found another type of service: they became our eyes. That year the Seeing Eye, the oldest Seeing Eye dog training school in the world, graduated its first two students in the United States— Gala and Tartar. The school was the brainchild of Frank Morris.

260

Mme L.C. de Liniers: Chien de la Société Nationale du chien sanitaire découvrant un blessé.

A French ambulance dog alerts near a fallen World War I soldier.

As a blind, twenty-year-old student at Vanderbilt University, Morris learned of dogs being trained in Switzerland to help blind people navigate their world. He was able to travel there and obtain a dog named Buddy. When the two returned to the United States, Morris wanted to share the newfound freedom he had gained with others who were blind. He began a school in Tennessee that would change the lives of blind people in the United States and inspire the use of dogs in many other service areas.

Who would think that almost a century later we would hear about a See-ing Eye dog named Roselle who would guide her master out of one of the world's worst disasters—the terrorist attack on the World Trade Center in 2001. Roselle guided Michael Hingson down seventy-eight floors in Tower One after American Airlines Flight 11 crashed into the building just eight-een floors above him. Roselle's determination, training, and bond with her master enabled the two of them to escape and help others along the way.

The bonds we share with dogs shout out at us from movies and the pages of books. Lassie and Rin Tin Tin became famous household names in the 1950s and 1960s. How many tears have been shed reading about Old Yeller, Sounder, or Shiloh since then?

And there are the dogs we read about in our history books such as Balto, the Siberian husky sled dog that led his team fifty-three miles (85.3 kilo-meters) to deliver medicine to Nome, Alaska. Did you know that the most well-known dog name, Fido, is derived from the Latin word *fidelis*, mean-ing "faithful"? President Lincoln named his dog Fido. Another Fido, in Italy, went to the bus station every day and waited for his master to return from work. One fateful day, during World War II, his master didn't return. But

Fido returned to the place for the next fourteen years, looking for his master. A statue of the faithful little dog still stands in a piazza near Florence, Italy.

Although not named Fido, Greyfriars Bobby in Scotland and Hachiko in Japan are two more dogs that remained faith-ful to their owners for many years after their mas-

Alan, a medical detection dog, is on the job. ↓

← Bill McGovern and K9 Braith and John Fairclough and K9 Ashes. Combined, these accelerant detection teams have worked on more than 225 fire searches.

ters' deaths. Both are now immortalized in statues (and in books and movies) for the loyal bond they shared with their owners. Even more recent is the story of an Argentinean dog, Capitan, who has stood guard over his master's grave since 2006. What is even more unusual about the story is that, even though Capitan had never been to the cemetery where Miguel Guzman is buried, he found his grave. Could he have sniffed his way there?

Dogs form a bridge for us to the natural world. Their relation to wolves and coyotes creates an animal that is both wild and tame. They guard. They guide. They are our companions. They help us hunt. And *they sniff*.

Nowadays many dogs work beside us to enrich our lives. They use their incredible sense of smell to help find us, keep us safe, and rescue us from danger. They even help protect the planet.

All of these dogs undergo training for their jobs. They provide their handlers with "alerts"—these could be a bark; a posture, such as sitting down or lying at their handler's feet; or a nudge to the knee. Each job requires a different alert and different skill set. But all their jobs require the power to sniff. We've heard of movie stars and singers insuring their body parts; well, a dog's nose can't be insured—it's priceless.

Whatever you call them—dogs, pooches, canines, pups, bow-wows—they are more than our "best friends"; they are often our sniffing heroes, letting their noses lead the way to feats of heroism.

THE SCIENCE OF SNIFFING

Gatsby steps outside with me for a walk. The dog quickly sniffs the air, the ground, and the bushes. I smell only the sweet scent of the lilacs blooming nearby. But Gatsby smells everything. He smells not only the blooming lilacs, but also the squirrel that ran up the pine tree that morning, the deer that wandered through the garden, the cat that crossed the driveway, the moth that landed on a flower, the place where he pooped the day before, and the pizza I picked up in my car last night. His nose takes it all in. Smell upon smell upon smell.

A dog's nose, unlike ours, doesn't just pick up the strongest scent in a room or a yard. Dogs smell *every* scent. Sort of like the way we hear. We can walk into a room and hear lots of different sounds in one place: the voices on the television, a dishwasher running, and the click-clack of fingers on a computer keyboard. When a dog walks into that same room it not only hears everything, but is able to smell everything too—the cat that just darted by, the candy wrapper you threw away in the garbage, the dirty clothes on the floor of your closet,

Gatsby: goldendoodle, three-year-old amateur sniffer.

and the dog you petted at your friend's house. How do they do it?

↑ Dogs classified as scenthounds by the American Kennel Club include bloodhounds (such as this one), beagles, and basset hounds. They are the strongest sniffers among canines.

A dog's nose has hundreds of millions of sensory neurons just waiting to process that next scent, approximately three hundred million or more to a human's lowly six million. All those neurons help make their sense of smell roughly 1,000 to 10,000 times greater than ours. In other words, if our vision were as powerful as a dog's scent ability, we would be able to see the small letters on an eye chart from about four miles (6.4 kilometers) away!

Gatsby is a mixed-breed dog, half poodle and half English golden retriever. He's a great sniffer, but some breeds rise to the level of super sniff-ers. Bloodhounds, for example, are sometimes called "a nose with a dog attached" because their sense of smell is one of the strongest among all dog breeds.

Have you ever seen a bloodhound? Even its face is designed to enhance its sense of smell. The dog's drooping, long ears wrap around its nose and drag along the ground collecting odors, and loose, floppy wrinkles on its face help trap scent particles. Bloodhounds are so adept at using their sense of smell that they have been known to fol-low a scent for over a hundred miles (161 kilome-ters), even while bombarded by other odors.

Dogs have the amazing ability to smell past,

Buford, a Southern Pride bloodhound, is extra-ordinary, even at the age of two. He's a persistent tracker. On one search he jumped off a cliff and knocked himself out. When he came to, he went on following the trail with his same enthusiasm. ↓

present, and future. They can differentiate between the strong smell of an animal's fresh urine and the fainter smell of urine that's a few days old. They can sniff a telephone pole and know which dogs, male or female, have visited it and when. They can also pick up on a breeze the scent of a person or animal who is walking toward them but not yet in sight.

Even if we got down on all fours and put our nose close to the ground, we couldn't begin to have the same experience as a dog. Our nose is just not built like theirs. Have you ever watched your dog sniff the air? Gatsby's nostrils move and pulse, drawing air in. Our less specialized sniffing nose is designed for the air to enter our nostrils in one motion and exit through the same nostrils in another. We inhale, and then exhale. Not so for a dog. Muscles in the nostrils draw in the air. When a dog sniffs the air, scent particles travel into the nasal cavity with the rushing air. This also happens to us, but in a dog, the air already in the dog's nose is forced deeper back into the nasal cavity. This movement creates tiny wind currents that help pull in more scent as air is exhaled.

Once inside the nose, mucus traps the scent particles and millions of receptors begin to process them, just like data being entered into a computer. Chemical signals are sent to a part of the dog's brain called the olfactory bulb, where they're analyzed. The dog's brain forms a sort of image identifying the smell. This "image" is even better than a photograph. A photo provides only visual clues to identify something or someone, but this "image" in the dog's brain provides even more sensory clues, including where someone's

NASAL CAVITY

been and the person's health condition. From that "image" the dog has enough clues to help it follow that scent to its owner.

Think about how we humans learn about the world around us. The cognitive scientist Alexandra Horowitz uses the example of a rose to describe the difference in how dogs and humans gather information. Humans will observe the color and shape of the flower.

↑ As well as having millions of neurons, a dog's nose has an additional organ to help it smell, the Jacobson's organ.

Dogs will take a whiff and smell the distinctive scent of each rose. A dog gains different information from its sniffing investigation. "Each petal on a rose may be distinct, having been visited by insects leaving pollen footprints from faraway places," Horowitz says. While humans "see one of the petals drying and browning, the dog can smell this process of decay and aging."

Sniffing is the best way for a dog to gather information. Scents go directly from nose to brain. Dogs can detect scent concentration levels at one to two parts per trillion, meaning that a dog can detect one to two scent molecules among a trillion molecules of air. In comparison, a shark, considered the super sniffer of the ocean, can detect only one drop of blood in a billion parts of ocean water.

To a dog even his human best friend is mostly scent. As you know, dogs

It's a myth that dogs can't see color. They do, except they see color differently than humans. Their color spectrum is limited. Humans have three different cone cells in the retina of the eye that are color sensitive. These cells enable us to see the full red-green-blue color spectrum. A dog has only two color-sensitive cone cells, green and blue. Scientists have determined that their vision is similar to that of someone who suffers from red-green colorblindness. A dog can see a rose, but it appears to be a shade of yellow instead of red. On the other hand, violets still appear a shade of blue.

can't wait to come up to us and take a sniff (sometimes in the most inappropriate places). But that is just their way of confirming our identification. As humans, we perspire, or sweat. Each of us has our own special sweat aroma, like a fingerprint. And even if we haven't been out running a marathon, our bodies still emit perspiration. Dogs can smell it well before we can.

For humans, the sense of smell goes hand in hand with memory. We walk through a forest, take a deep breath, and are brought back to a Christmas tree glistening in our living room. We can remember the smell of pancakes cooking on a griddle even if we're far from a kitchen. Imagine if our noses were as keen as a dog's.

As Gatsby sleeps he twitches, whimpers, and sniffs. Is he dreaming? What memories does he have? What do his smells trigger as he sleeps?

When we are angry or upset, our sweat contains chemicals called pheromones. Dogs can smell those too. Dogs are indeed sensitive to our emotions. Have you ever heard that dogs can smell fear? It's true. They can smell chemicals, such as adrenaline, that our body produces when we're fearful. The chemicals in our body rise more quickly to the surface of the skin when we're afraid, making it even easier for a dog to read our feelings. They not only smell the new odor we create, but also recognize the change from the way we smelled before we experienced that feeling.

But we are more than the smell of sweat to a dog. The human body is covered with skin. Our skin sheds tiny cells all the time that are invisible to the human eye. We leave skin cells behind on everything we touch. Dogs can't see them, but they can certainly smell them. They know where we've been. Dogs can follow scents by sniffing the ground for scent molecules, which is known as tracking; or, if they're air-scent dogs, by sniffing the air (known as trailing).

Ella, a black Labrador retriever, is a hunting dog. She is trained to help sniff and flush out birds from the fields, but on this occasion she watches her master throw a tennis ball into the woods. It's not a bird, but Ella is used to this game too. The ball lands among the green and yellow autumn leaves, out of everyone's sight. Ella isn't relying on her sight, however. Her nose leads her to the ball. Once she's picked up its scent, she follows the scent molecules that are dispersing from the source in a cone formation. Ella disappears into the brush.

Imagine a cone shape, with the point of the cone being the source of the scent. As Ella picks up the scent in her nose, she starts to zigzag back and forth in the scent cone, getting closer and closer to the point of the cone, the tennis ball. It is amazing to watch her speed as she moves away from the edge of the scent cone and instantly turns back into it. Handlers call this being in odor and out odor. Susannah Charleson, an author and search and rescue (SAR) handler, likens the process to

> A search dog will zig and zag to the edges of the cone until reaching the origin of the scent.

playing the game of hot and cold. As the dog moves into the scent cone, it gets "warmer" (closer to the ball). As it moves to the edge and out of the cone, it gets "colder."

Despite what you might think, a strong gust of wind can help a scent cone become narrow and focused. The dog doesn't have to zigzag so much to stay inside it. It can almost run straight to the source. If the wind is slight, the scent cone is wider, because the molecules dissipate slowly over a greater area. The dog has to run a little bit more to pinpoint the scent. It takes only a few minutes for Ella to locate her ball. She emerges from the brush, tail wagging, body wriggling, ball in mouth. Everyone claps!

The movement of scent molecules can be demonstrated by watching the colored smoke from a smoke bomb release and drift. The smoke will act just like scent molecules as it hangs among the trunks of trees or drifts along the ground.

Both tracking dogs and trailing dogs are given something to smell that contains the scent of the person or thing it needs to find. A tracking dog, such as a bloodhound, will then put its nose to the ground and sniff as it moves along the path the scent has left behind. It will follow actual footprints. Scientists have determined

Ella: eight-year-old black Labrador, hunting dog, on the job for seven years.

Nose to the ground, this bloodhound sniffs her way to locate a "missing" person in a training exercise.

that it takes a dog only five footsteps to determine the direction of the scent trail left by a human.

A trailing dog will keep its nose to the air and smell the scent that collects on vegetation, fences, or trees as the scent molecules drift away from the source. In that case, the dog isn't following the scent on the ground, but

↑ Watch your dog's nostrils pulse as they draw scent into the nose.

rather following the scent trail the human leaves as the person continues to move.

Sometimes the search is for a specific person whose scent is not known. For example, the "missing" person could be a fugitive, attempting to escape police custody. Police have used "live-find" dogs for more than a century to track suspects. According to Dr. Robert H. Wright, noted olfaction researcher and author of *The Sense of Smell,* when a dog is asked to "find him" at the scene of a crime and the suspect's scent is not known, the dog "will be tracking a particular kind of man, namely one in a special emotional state." Dogs can be successful working with or without a known scent. They can smell the individual's heightened perspiration and the chemicals, such as adrenaline, the body emits in that situation. They can follow that scent from the scene of a crime and track it to the hiding individual.

Both tracking and trailing dogs, usually working on a lead, or leash, can be used to find missing persons or police suspects. Air-scent dogs are used more often, off-lead, to find unknown people trapped in disasters and to assist conservation scientists in the field.

Many other animals have a keen sense of smell, but no others have proven to be as useful and loyal as the dog. Pigs can find the rare and delicious mushrooms called truffles that grow underground. Seabirds can navigate using their sense of smell. Great white sharks can smell one drop of a substance, such as blood from their potential dinner, in a billion parts of seawater. But can those animals use their sense of smell to help rescue humans after a building collapse? Or use their sense of smell to detect trace amounts of explosives? Or smell the change in blood sugar in an infant? Only dogs can do that.

Whether they are sniffing for a person, an explosive, an accelerant, or another animal's scat, dogs constantly amaze us with their sniffing abilities. ↓

LIVE-FIND SNIFFERS

The game begins. Raider, a Labrador/border collie mix, knows that his handler, Sara Rathbun, has his toy behind her back. Sara, a Los Angeles firefighter, instructs Raider to climb the round-rung ladder in front of him. Without hesitation, Raider proceeds off-lead up the slippery rungs. They're difficult to climb with his wide paws, but he continues. If this were an actual deployment, this ladder might be the only way in to reach people trapped in flames, smoke, or a collapsed building. Raider moves along, one rung at a time, until he reaches the top.

Sara calls him back down. This is a test of his agility and willingness to search. All new live-find search dogs must pass this test and others to become certified by FEMA. Slowly, Raider makes his way headfirst down the ladder. Rung after rung, one at a time. Finally, he's down, and Sara is there waiting with both praise and his toy.

His tail wags. Success! He grabs the rubber toy and tugs with Sara.

Raider climbs up a ladder, another "junk agility" test. The handlers use seesaws, ladders, planks, and tubes to help the dogs develop the skill set they'll use when on "the pile" during an actual deployment. →

If this were an actual disaster, the hoots and hollering praise for Raider's accomplishment at finding a victim would surpass all the praise he's received during training.

Raider and Sara became a certified FEMA search team in June of 2012. They are one of ten active teams out of the LA/Northnet Training Group, which is one of two international deployable task forces in the United States. Like the other teams on the task force, they receive training and support from the National Disaster Search Dog Foundation, founded by Wilma Melville.

When Wilma, a retired physical education teacher, "wanted to learn to train a dog to do something special," she began a path that would change the lives of many Americans. She and her black Labrador, Murphy, became a certified FEMA search and rescue team. But Wilma didn't stop there.

When Wilma and Murphy were deployed to find survivors after the terrorist bombing of the Alfred P. Murrah Federal Building in Oklahoma City in 1995, she discovered that there were only fifteen FEMA-certified search teams in the country. This was not nearly enough for the entire United States, and although the teams did rescue one victim, handlers were frustrated that there were not enough teams

Raider: three-year-old border collie/Labrador mix, search and rescue

Potential live-find dogs are given a toy when they bark at initial trainings. Once the dogs know that they will receive their toy when they bark, the handlers/trainers hide with the toy and release it to the dog when the dog locates them and barks. The game goes on until the dog realizes it will receive the toy when it finds a live human and barks its alert. Who needs a paycheck when you can play tug?

Firefighter Sara Rathbun and her teammate, Raider.

to cover the entire site. The following year, Wilma founded the National Disaster Search Dog Foundation to create more search and rescue teams.

Wilma was not only beginning her own second career; she was about to give countless dogs a second chance, too. About 90 percent of live-find search dogs were once abandoned at animal shelters, often termed useless or unmanageable by their original owners. Raider was one of those dogs.

"He was literally on death row," says Sara. It's hard to believe now, but Raider was considered unadoptable. He would have met a very different fate if not for the workers from the Oregon Humane Society, who found him at a kill shelter in northern California. They recognized him as a potential live-find dog and brought him to the Search Dog Foundation (SDF).

They were right; Raider is a typical live-find dog. He's toy-obsessed, high energy, athletic, and always willing to work. "He's frenetic," says Sara. "He can't sit still." Even after a morning of training in the hot desert sun, Raider keeps pacing around the room.

He was difficult to work with at first. Sara had to find a balance with him. He strived to be dominant, like many search dogs, challenging his handler at every turn. Sara wanted to make him the best search dog possible. It took a lot of work and many repetitions. But watching him at training, Sara is like a proud mom. "He's amazing on the pile," she says. The "pile" Sara refers to is the debris that the dogs practice on to get them ready for a real pile—the stacks of concrete, wood, and debris that make up the remains of a collapsed building.

↑ Raider waits for his next command after climbing a ladder during training.

Wilma speaks highly of these rescued live-find dogs. "They have drive. They have boldness. They have self-confidence."

The SDF has trained over a hundred dogs and teamed them up with firefighters throughout the United States. The dogs are provided food, health insurance to cover their medical bills, and ongoing training for the rest of their search and rescue career. The foundation's teams have experienced more than seventy-seven deployments, including many high-profile disasters, such as the World Trade Center and Pentagon tragedies; the 2011 tornado in Joplin, Missouri; and the horrendous earthquakes of Haiti in 2010 and Japan in 2011.

"There is nothing better than a dog's nose to find a live human," says Wilma. Once a dog locates a survivor it provides its handler with a bark alert to let the handler know it has found someone.

Where we rely on sight and sound, a dog uses its sense of smell, which is much more efficient in the rubble of these disasters. Dogs can find someone hidden in the remains of a building, unconscious and quiet. They can get into nooks and crannies and search in places a human can't. And they never stop searching.

"A search dog will smell everyone in their sight and then, when they smell an additional human, they go look for the one that is missing," says Sara.

"The beauty of the dogs is that they give people hope that someone can be found alive," says Wilma.

Another handler, Shirley Hammond, was with Wilma on the scene of the Oklahoma City bombing. Shirley and her husband, David, a retired structural engineer, had taken part in many other deployments before the federal building in Oklahoma City was bombed. Her red Doberman, Cinnamon, had accompanied her to Mexico ten years earlier, in 1985, when Mexico City experienced a devastating earthquake. At that time, Shirley was a volunteer with the California Rescue Dog Association.

The dogs were trained in the Swiss rescue format—avalanche, wilderness, and disaster. Cinnamon was already disaster and wilderness trained when she and Shirley were lowered into the remains of a fourteen-story clothing factory in Mexico City where a neighborhood cook had thought he heard the sounds of human moaning.

A crane lifted the team onto the roof of the collapsed building. Shirley, treating her dog as her partner, told Cinny what was going to happen. Shirley would go down first. Cinnamon would be handed down "worker by worker" into a shaft created by the rescue team until she got down to

the bottom of the factory building. "Workers had made a hole with their shovels, like a well," says Shirley.

↑ Lani on the pile during a disaster training.

Shirley, with hardhat and knee pads, crawled on hands and knees with her dog between the collapsed floors to search for anyone alive after the quake. About ten minutes later an aftershock occurred. Debris and dust fell down around them. The dog didn't stop. Cinnamon scampered over the rubble with Shirley following cautiously behind her.

A dog's agility often enables it to move more quickly than its handlers. Cinnamon was no exception. When Shirley caught up with her dog, she found Cinnamon on her stomach, digging, trying in vain to remove the rubble. Then came her alert. Bark! Bark!

"We knew that there were people there," says Shirley. Cinnamon could smell them. The rescue workers began to dig in that spot. Shirley praised Cinnamon and they moved on to search for others. Who knew how many more victims might be waiting to be rescued? Live-find search teams don't have the luxury to wait and see if their efforts are successful. Time is of the essence. Minutes can make a difference between life and death for the trapped victims of a disaster.

Cinnamon and Shirley moved on to other areas, but the Doberman did not sniff out any other victims. Shirley didn't know if anyone was found

Like wolves, dogs prefer to live in social groups called packs. If you own a dog, your family becomes your dog's pack. In any group there is a leader. The leader in a dog pack is known as the alpha. The alpha dog is dominant, but that doesn't mean aggressive. However, that status does produce demanding and pushy behavior, as the dog constantly tests its boundaries, which may lead to a bad relationship in the family. Trainers strive to instruct dogs to be submissive to their human alpha leader, who in turn becomes a gentle authority figure. Search and rescue dogs are taught with the same training methods that work with your family dog, except that many SAR dogs naturally strive to be dominant.

alive in the factory building that day until they were ready to board the plane back to the United States. "An embassy person came out and told us that they had pulled ten live people out of there," said Shirley.

Cinnamon and Shirley had risked their lives to save those people. "Only afterwards do you realize the situation you've been in," says Shirley.

After the Mexico City disaster, the number of search dogs in the United States increased. When the terrorist attack of September 11, 2001, rocked the United States, Shirley answered the call again. So did many of the other teams Wilma had trained. Search and rescue teams arrived in New York City at the site of the World Trade Center, now known as Ground Zero.

Shirley's Task Force 3 from Menlo Park, California, deployed with four dogs to the site of the disaster. Twenty of FEMA's twenty-eight urban search and rescue teams came from all over to help search with dogs through the debris, but many more volunteers with dogs also came to help. Not all were trained to locate trapped people, but their handlers were there to help at the massive site. They worked tirelessly amid the noise of heavy rescue machinery and the smell of smoke and decomposing bodies.

"It was like nothing I had ever seen in my life," says Shirley. "It was almost like a movie set, but it was so real. There was still so much burning."

The site was difficult for everyone. "The gas masks that the searchers were supposed to wear came on and off because you couldn't communicate with the dog through the mask," says Shirley, her voice breaking as she recalled the difficult days she spent there.

Live-find dogs are trained to detect traces of human sweat and other musky odors our bodies produce in times of stress. Dog handlers from Maryland's Task Force Rescue Team believed that even the dogs felt the same frustration the handlers experienced at not finding many live people in the debris. Some of the rescuers even held mock rescues, hiding themselves among the rubble to provide the dogs with the satisfaction and hope of a find. In return the dogs provided comfort for their handlers.

Shirley had another dog by then, Sunny, a male Doberman that weighed about ninety

↑ Shirley Hammond and Sunny during their deployment at the World Trade Center in September 2001.

pounds (40.8 kilograms). Like all search dogs, he was trained to bark an alert to his handler. When he did bark on the site, Shirley got excited. But soon her hopes were dashed as they discovered the "victim" Sunny had located

was actually a New York task force worker tunneling to get someplace in the debris. Although it gave Sunny a boost, it was not what Shirley was expecting.

Her saddest moment came when Sunny was able to direct firefighters to one of their deceased "brothers." Sunny had trained in an area where human remains detection dogs had also trained and recognized the scent of human decomposition. But he was trained only to find live humans. His alert was confused. Should he bark? Or sit? Or spin around? The scent did not come from a living human, but it was a familiar scent. He had to tell his handler, but wasn't sure how. Shirley understood his mixed signals and alerted the firefighters to the area. The firefighters were grateful the dog was able to assist in their search, even though the outcome was terribly sad.

Genelle Guzman began her day in the North Tower of the World Trade Center on September 11, 2001. She was chatting with her coworker when a plane hit the tower. The building shook. She was knocked to the floor as everything rumbled around her, filling the air with dust and pinning her body to the debris. Only her left arm was free from piles of concrete and steel. She tried to call out for help, but the dust clogged her throat. For twenty-seven long, painful hours, Genelle lay trapped under the debris.

According to two rescue workers, if not for an eight-year-old German shepherd named Trakr, Genelle's name would have been among the thousands listed in the Trade Center Memorial. Genelle was the last person rescued from the rubble of the tower collapse. Trakr's handler, Officer James Symington, and his friend, Cpl. John Hall, traveled down from Nova Scotia, Canada, to help in the rescue efforts following the attacks of September 11. The rescuers and the dogs were feeling frustrated and depressed by the lack of survivors when Trakr became intent on a pile of rubble. His handlers alerted the emergency crews and moved on to try to locate others. No others were found. Trakr had located the last survivor, number 20, thirty-two-year-old Genelle Guzman.

Each disaster burns in the memory of its rescue workers. It's hard to imagine that the dogs and handlers are able to continue after facing such devastation, but they do. Many, like Shirley, volunteer over and over again. Other search and rescue workers watch the handlers with their dogs and, by their next call, they have a dog of their own.

Before receiving Raider, Sara Rathbun of the Los Angeles Fire Department had been deployed to Japan following the earthquake and tsunami disaster in 2011. She saw how fast and efficient the search dogs there moved off-lead from building to building, rubble pile to rubble pile.

"The amount of ground they can cover is amazing," she said. "The dogs

A search dog is calmly transported above the wreckage during the search and rescue operations at the World Trade Center site. Detection dogs are trained to ride in all sorts of ways, including in elevators, helicopters, and hoists like the this one. →

there could probably clear the buildings a hundred times faster than I could. The feeling of helplessness and fear of leaving someone behind was mitigated. It was so much easier, faster, and more efficient to have these dogs on hand than to try and do it on my own."

These dogs train as though they are super athletes. Handlers must keep their dogs physically fit to be able to work each deployment, whatever the conditions—even though they never know when that deployment will happen.

"On any given day, that could be the day that he has to give his Olympic performance," says Sara about Raider. The dogs must be prepared at

Two search dogs wait their turn for the next training exercise. ↓

any time to face the harsh conditions of deployment, which might involve strenuous climbing, heat, snow, or long hours.

Even though these dogs are certified by FEMA, not all of their deployments are catastrophic national or international disasters. They might be sent with their handlers to the scene of a mudslide, an avalanche, or a car crash—anywhere a victim might need to be located. At the scene of a structure fire, a search dog can enter a building more easily than a firefighter wearing all his equipment. They are much lighter and can crawl into small spaces. For this reason, live-find dogs search without a vest, which can get hung up on the sharp objects and debris. Once the firefighters hear a bark, they know it's worth it to risk their lives and enter the building themselves.

On the afternoon of April 23, 2009, a fifteen-year-old girl with shoulder-length brown hair went missing from the YMCA in Glenville, New York. Within an hour 150 people were searching for her. At 6:30 that evening SDF's New York Search Teams were called in to help. Among them was Kura, a seven-year-old yellow Labrador/golden retriever. She was on the job with her handler, firefighter Greg Gould.

The search went on for hours, scouring the wooded and residential areas around the YMCA. Helicopters circled overhead.

Kura and her handler were sent to search the Oak Hill School, where the girl had attended class earlier that day. It was dark, and the two were met by other firefighters who claimed the area was already cleared. The search team manager, Tony Santulli, decided they should check the area again.

Greg sent Kura on her way. The calm, peaceful dog jumped into high gear. She ripped through the building, knocking down chairs and kitchen items, her nose hard at work sniffing. She headed up a flight of stairs. Minutes later Greg could hear Kura's feet jumping up and down with excitement followed by barking. He knew Kura had found someone. He headed upstairs. Sure enough, Kura and her nose were successful. The girl was found hiding deep inside a closet, alive and safe. At 10:23 p.m. the search ended, thanks to Kura and Greg.

↑ Kura was originally selected for the Canine Companions for Independence program but she had the high energy and drive of a search dog. She became Greg Gould's teammate in 2005.

Raider and Sara met Greg at the 2012 Iron Dog Competition, which took place in upstate New York. The annual event combines skills competition and training. It is set up by the Search Dog Foundation and takes place over a weekend. SAR dogs fly in from all over the country to participate. Raider and Sara were part of a four-dog search team that placed second, coming in with the most "finds"—fifteen out of sixteen! The team would probably have placed first if Raider and Sara hadn't had to sit out the agility

New York Task Force 2 with trainer Pluis Davern. Left to right: Pluis Davern and Lani, John Stewart and Sadi, Marsi and Bill Childs, filling in for Jason Geary, Greg Gould and Dax, and Bill Simmes and Bonnie. ↓

test because Raider had cut his pads on both front feet. SAR dogs are always susceptible to injuries like this in their dangerous working conditions. In fact, often volunteer veterinarians are at disaster sites to take care of the canines.

There are many volunteer search and rescue workers, but most are firefighters. Jasmine Segura was eighteen when she walked into a firehouse and was greeted at the door by a female firefighter. Seeing a woman in that position changed her life! Now she is a captain for the Los Angeles Fire Department and the handler for Raider's teammate. Her black Labrador, Cadillac, is almost ready for retirement.

Cadillac has had an amazing career. The two deployed to Haiti in 2010 after an earthquake ravaged the island. Along with other search teams trained by the Search Dog Foundation, Cadillac and Jasmine helped locate twelve trapped people. They also traveled to Japan as part of Sara Rathbun's team to help locate survivors in the wreckage of the 2011 tsunami disaster.

But like all athletes', a SAR dog's

Kura: now eleven years old, retired and living happily with her handler's family.

I'm crouched behind a pine tree in a North Carolina forest waiting patiently for Lex, a mixed-breed live-find dog, to locate me. The handler waited and let me get settled before releasing him. Before I left on my hike into the woods, the handler gave me a tissue to wipe the back of my neck. I had just applied bug spray, but no matter; my skin cells and scent would still come off

on the tissue for Lex to smell. After I'm in the woods about a half mile (.8 kilometer), Lex is allowed to sniff the tissue and is then released to find me. The woods are quiet except for the occasional bird whistle. And then I hear it—the bell on Lex's collar! He's on his way. It gets louder. I peer around the base of the tree and see him running through the woods. He's picked up my scent. He runs to the hill to my right and takes another sniff. I can see him. His handler is following him. Then he turns sharply toward me and runs full speed over the leaves and twigs. In seconds I'm greeted with a lick and he takes off again to "tell" his handler. I watch as the two scramble toward me. I'm found!

strength and endurance cannot last forever. Most handlers acquire their dog when it is two to four years old. The dog is certified for a three-year term. After that, handlers recertify their dog for another three years. At ten years old, the dog winds down for retirement. Some large dogs suffer the effects of the difficult job even earlier and retire at eight or nine.

At retirement, the days of crawling over rubble and climbing ladders end. The dogs, like Kura and Cadillac, retire to their handler's home to live out the rest of their lives as privileged pets. Even though they live with their handlers during their working career, their handlers do not own the dogs until the dogs are retired.

From shelter dog to blue-collar rescue worker to treasured pet. Not a bad journey.

Even though this search dog might want to continue along the training plank, she's commanded to the down position. ↓

BONE SNIFFERS

It's a Sunday morning in North Carolina and a group of cars pulls up at a state park. The people who emerge from the vehicles might look like they're there for a walk with their dogs, and they are, but their dogs aren't your usual Sunday morning strollers. They are detection dogs. Their handlers don't work together. They belong to different detection teams, but they train the dogs together twice a week to improve their skills and keep them sharp.

Loki, a black and white border collie, jumps out of his handler's SUV. He's a human remains detection (HRD) dog who's also cross-trained as a live-find dog. The majority of human remains detection dogs are search dogs schooled to ignore the scent of living humans and animals and focus only on the task of finding the remains of nonliving humans. Loki, however, works to find humans dead or alive.

Finding deceased people is an emotional job for any law enforcement official, but Loki and the other HRD dogs are up for it. The dogs assist the Federal Bureau of Investigation (FBI), police, and other agencies in locating victims at suspected crime scenes, airplane crash sites, and other disasters.

The dogs recognize decomposing body odors as the scent drifts away from the body or skeleton by way of diffusion, animal or insect activity, water movement, or the growth activity of roots and plants.

Loki is going to practice today on locating a container holding a piece of decomposing human flesh. The items the handlers use for training purposes are donated by individuals and are shared

among the handlers for increasing the scent library of their dogs.

The scent of decomposition changes from the moment a person dies and depends on all sorts of conditions. The scent of a body in the water is different from that in a fire or in the heat of a summer day. The scent changes each day as the body continues to decompose. It helps if the dog has some familiarity with the different scents of decomposition. Trainers work to increase a dog's scent library so that the dog can draw on it when they are searching. Trainings help increase that library and the scope of what they can detect.

These dogs are trained only in locating human remains. Building their familiarity with human decomposition odors of various stages and circumstances also helps reinforce what they are asked to locate. When released, they will go about their job and ignore any animal remains that might be in their path.

Loki gets the command "Seek." He runs off into the woods, off-lead, to search for human scent. The vial has been hidden in a mound, covered with leaves and pine needles. It doesn't take Loki more than a few minutes to pick up its scent. He circles around the area, running an inventory in his mind of everything he smells. He scratches at the earth to bring up more scent.

His handler, Don, asks, "Is that it, Loki?" The

Loki sniffs out the vial of decomposing flesh hidden by the handlers. ↓

scent is similar but not exactly the same as his previous finds, but it is similar enough. The dog barks and runs back to him. Loki practices a re-find alert, meaning he barks, runs back to his handler, and brings his handler back to the spot to show him what he's found. Don follows Loki. When they reach the spot, the dog exhibits a "down" alert that resembles the pose of an Egyptian sphinx, and he is rewarded with his toy.

Loki has now added another scent to his library. He'll remember that smell when he's on an actual job.

Dogs can find missing bodies. But can dogs be trained to find very old bones, bones that have been buried for possibly hundreds of years?

No one knew until Adela Morris was with her search dog near a cemetery in the mid-1990s. Curious, she put her dog over the fence and, to her amazement, the dog started to alert at every grave. She knew she had something special. In 1997, Adela founded the Institute for Canine Forensics (ICF). The institute is the only group focused on historic human remains detection. The ICF now has twelve handlers and fifteen dogs ready for deployment to locate bones that could be hundreds of years old—even mummified remains. How do the dogs detect very old bones?

Loki: in service with handler Donald Lysle for human remains detection and search and rescue.

You might find it hard to believe that it can actually be easier for dogs to locate buried bones than bones exposed on the surface of the ground. The reason is that surface bones have a greater chance of breaking down and losing their scent over time in the sunlight, wind, and heat. Bones buried in undisturbed graves have less chance of breaking down and a greater chance of retaining their scent. The soil around a decomposed body retains the human signature that the dogs are trained to locate.

The dogs rely on the release of subtle odors that escape to the ground's surface in a number of ways. For example, rainwater penetrates the ground and washes over the remains. Chemical compounds from the decomposition of the body are transported with the flow of water. Scent molecules, like water, take the path of least resistance and flow with the water or air currents. As water molecules evaporate to the surface or flow to a new location, the scent moves with them and is released. Burrowing animals, such as ground squirrels and moles, as well as some insects, create channels in the soil that scent molecules can follow to the surface.

According to Lynne Angeloro, vice president of the Institute for Canine Forensics, "The dogs can find human remains down to approximately six to nine feet (2–3 meters), but this is very dependent upon the ground consistency—clay, sand, or loamy soils—moisture, and ground and air temperature."

Dogs selected for the ICF must have the temperament and drive to become specialized in this type of search and recovery. The most successful

Zuma: seven-year-old border collie, alerting since she was five weeks old, historic human remains detection professional

dogs will find a bone, move into a down alert, and go off to find another. The ICF trains many types of dogs, including border collies, Australian shepherds, and retrievers.

ICF dogs are trained specifically to find old bones and are rarely trained for any other type of detection work. Lynne Angeloro says, "If you teach the dog the big scent of big decomposition, it's difficult to then teach the subtle smell of buried bones."

"Berkley can find a tooth in an acre in less than two minutes if the conditions are right," says Lynne of her two-and-a-half-year-old red and white border collie.

Zuma, another red and white border collie, is also a specialist at finding teeth. This serious seven-year-old's abilities were tested when she was asked to locate ten human teeth in a horse pasture filled with smelly horse manure, live horses, and the remains of local animals. Amid all those distractions and nonhuman scents, Zuma succeeded. She was even able to smell the difference between human and nonhuman teeth.

Her trainer, Donna Randolph, releases her from her crate for her turn at searching this Sunday morning. Before her first search begins, she's walked.

"It's important to be respectful of an area," says Donna. ICF dogs are often brought into sensitive areas, such as old cemeteries or crime scenes. Walking them before they enter the search area keeps the search area clean of any "deposits." Once Zuma is finished she's ready for her first "problem."

The handlers have placed a dime-size sprinkling of "cremains" into the dirt and tamped it down so that the dogs don't inhale any of it when they are sniffing. Cremains are human remains that have been cremated to a temperature of 6,000°F (3,315°C) and then pulverized to a sandlike consistency with small bits of bone and teeth. It's hard to believe that there is any scent left at all after the process.

Zuma receives her command to search. Without knowing what she is searching for, the small dog walks slowly, deliberately, off-lead, nose to the

Zuma searches the ground after getting her search command from Donna. All trainers use their own commands for their dogs. ↓

ground. Donna follows from behind and watches her. Zuma reaches the spot of the remains and goes into a down alert. Donna praises her dog and throws her ball.

↑ Zuma exhibits her down alert without hesitation after locating a tiny bit of human cremation remains in the dirt.

Donna has had Zuma since she was a puppy and proudly tells the story of how Zuma began alerting at five weeks old. "The nose develops first, then the ears, then the eyes," says Donna. Zuma's nose has been working ever since. "Zuma loves to work because it gives us an opportunity to interact," says Donna. All the dogs have different personalities and different motivations.

"Now, Jax is different," says Donna. Jax, a nine-month-old red and white border collie, was a rescue dog. Donna has had him for a month and the training is going well. "Jax likes the discovery. He enjoys the mental stimulation of the search puzzle."

Jax is waiting for his time to search today, as it's still Zuma's turn. Zuma continues on into the woods where the handlers have hidden three human bones—a mandible, a rib bone, and a vertebra. The scent is much subtler than the fresh scent of the decomposing flesh Loki searched for, but Zuma is an expert. She methodically surveys the ground with her nose. She arrives at the first spot, where the rib bone has been wedged between the bases of two tree trunks. She moves into her down alert and looks at Donna for her approval.

"Good girl!" Donna rewards Zuma with a bit of play time—a throw of the ball and a brief game of tug of war with the attached rope. Bones can become distributed around an area as animals or elements move them from the decomposed body. Donna is familiar with that circumstance. She's been a handler for about twenty years. Zuma is her second dog.

"When they have that moment of discovery, it's so rewarding to see," she says, taking the ball again from Zuma and commanding her to continue searching. Zuma puts her nose to the ground and begins the next search. But the next is a little more difficult. She circles around a sapling and looks up, then circles again. The vertebra has been placed on a broken twig on the sapling. It's off the ground, not in the usual spot she would likely find her bones. You can hear the deep sniffs she is taking, drawing in all the information she can. Sometimes she sniffs so hard you can hear a popping sound in her nose. She looks up into the tree, stretches upward, and then begins

↑ Donna has placed a donated human vertebrae on a broken twig for the dogs to locate.

her down alert. It was difficult, but she knows the bone is up there.

Again she's praised and moves on to the next spot, which she quickly finds. It's the mandible, which has been placed under a log. Now it's Jax's turn. He locates the rib bone quickly, but is still learning the appropriate alert. Donna is firm as the dog extends his front paws down but keeps his back end raised. "Down," repeats Donna. As with all training, repetition and consistency are important. Finally, Jax is all the way down and receives his reward.

It's a beautiful autumn day this Sunday morning. The air is cool and clear. The temperature and conditions are important when training. Sometimes the handlers have to take the dogs out at first light to get the conditions right. If the ground temperature is too hot, it is difficult for these nose-to-ground searching dogs. When the temperature of the ground rises above 100°F (37.8°C), the dogs will have a difficult time picking up a scent. The ideal temperature range for the ground is between 45 and 80 degrees (7–27°C). Early-morning dew is ideal. The moisture freshens the scent and gives the dog a greater chance of sniffing more scent molecules. The moisture seems to create more scent, or rather, makes the scent more available to

Jax is quick to find bones, but his alert still needs work—he keeps his back end up with his front paws down, or he sits into a "half alert." Donna is firm as she commands him to a complete down position before moving on to his next search.

It is important for working dogs to travel safely to a training or deployment. Jax waits patiently in his crate for his turn at the game.

the dog. "We are not sure how or why. The moisture or morning dew helps transport the scent to the vegetation," says Donna.

The ICF dogs have found everything from unmarked family graves to ancient Native American burial sites. The oldest bones located by an ICF dog, dated to A.D. 450, were found in the Czech Republic. On the other side of the world, another dog, named Migaloo, is working with archaeologists to find historic bones in Australia. This Labrador retriever recently located a six-hundred-year-old Aboriginal burial site. Those are some old bones.

Not far from the redwoods and high peaks of Yosemite National Park is the largest unrestored ghost town in the country. Bodie became the fifth-largest town in California just twenty years after gold was discovered there in 1859. Boom years followed from 1879–82. Now it is a California state park, and visitors can wander the quiet, abandoned streets and peer into the windows of the empty schoolhouse.

Although population had dwindled in Bodie, most of the remaining residents left after a devastating fire in 1892 destroyed more than seventy percent of the town. The remaining buildings sit in eerie silence. The cemetery lies quiet and undisturbed. That is, it did until the dogs were called in. The dogs of the Institute of Canine Forensics were employed to search for the unmarked graves of Bodie's past residents.

Adela Morris pats the dog sitting at her feet and says, "This is a tool that is so unique. This can't be duplicated any other way. They [the park service] can't dig to find the burials. It is not permitted. This is the only tool that will work to look for some of these burials." The park service knew the cemetery held more than what was marked, but had no maps to follow. According to Terri Geissinger of the Bodie Foundation, the dogs located 295 unmarked graves within the fenced cemetery during their first year in the park.

"The first time I met the dogs, I met Tali. She alerted right away at the grave of the woman I portray at Bodie. I got so emotional. She connected in a way I couldn't," says Terri. That was about seven years ago.

They have a lot of work yet to do at Bodie. The dogs continue their work outside of the fenced cemetery and have located upwards of fifty additional unmarked graves during annual visits. They will keep returning as long as funding allows.

"At least we know there are bodies there so we can honor them and protect them in the future," says Terri.

The ICF handlers are trained to use maps and study the past. They are often called in when cemeteries need to be moved or mapped. They look for changes in the landscape before bringing in their dogs. They might find a depression in a later map that didn't exist earlier or other changes in the terrain that might indicate a disturbance.

"I love history," says Donna. "Tell me your story. Tell me your family's story."

Seeing Donna with Zuma and Jax, you would never know she didn't grow up with dogs. Her mom was terrified of them. Instead, she had horses. Duke, a mutt, became her first dog and, thanks to a meeting with Adela, her

The historic mining town of Bodie, California.

first detection dog. "Duke had drive," says Donna. "He needed something to do."

The ICF dogs never dig. They are trained to only sniff and alert, and not to touch anything they locate. They don't disturb the past; they only bring it to light. It is gratifying for a handler each time a dog alerts, but some jobs bring even more satisfaction.

The FBI and other law enforcement call in ICF teams to help with cold cases. A prison confession may lead to the location of a body that was disposed of decades earlier.

"Finding someone and giving their loved ones closure is so rewarding," says Lynne Angeloro.

Sometimes, however, a search yields surprises and the team locates the bones of someone else. After such slow and tedious work, it is frustrating when the case they are working on cannot be closed. "It's very disappointing when you're working out there for months and you find something that you weren't looking for," says Donna. It only opens up more questions for the ICF team and the authorities.

More often, though, the dogs are able to provide the closure that families need. In some instances, that closure comes many years after the death of a loved one.

In 2007, the dogs were called in to search for the remains of two missing World War II servicemen. The two men, a pilot and a gunner, were flying on a training mission when their plane went down near the Pajaro River in northern California. Sadly, the bodies of the airmen were never recovered. Decades later, remains of the plane were located by the Pajaro Water Management Agency during the construction of a new irrigation system. ICF dogs were able to locate many of the bones of the missing men at the site, including a finger bone with a ring on it. Family members of the fallen servicemen were contacted and a memorial was set up at the site of the crash to honor the airmen.

"There is no peace for these families until you have answers," says Lynne Angeloro.

These dogs help provide those answers.

On August 13, 2012, Diane Whetsel gave her border collie, Sage, her last command. She instructed her beloved human remains detection canine to cross what many call the rainbow bridge and go on to a life without pain and suffering. Diane couldn't go with her on this particular journey, as she had on so many others. The two had worked as a team on many missions. Diane was a gang officer in the Security Threat Intelligence unit at a corrections facility in New Mexico. When she became Sage's handler she had advanced certification as a K9 unit dog handler and was also a trainer.

"She was a skinny little spit of a thing. She had such a strong work drive that I needed to teach her a command to drink. She never wanted to take the time from her work," said Diane. Sage took part in the search and recovery efforts at the Pentagon after the terrorist attacks of 9/11. It was two-year-old Sage's first deployment and the light-as-a-cat dog proved invaluable amid the rubble. She was able to locate the body of the terrorist who flew the plane into the Pentagon.

A few years and many deployments later she was with Diane in Iraq, and Diane says Sage became as comfortable riding in Black Hawk helicopters as she was back home in the family car. Sage and Diane spent six months in Iraq, searching fields, farms, and industrial areas, anywhere soldiers had been ambushed.

When Sage wasn't out locating missing soldiers, she became a much-needed source of comfort to the troops. "She was there to lick a dirty face or play a game of Frisbee whenever there was time and a safe place to rest," says Diane. "She was a little piece of home for the soldiers."

It was no wonder Sage was one of the finalists in the 2011 American Humane Association's Hero Dog Awards and won in the category of Search and Rescue Dogs.

SNIFFING OUT EXPLOSIVES, NARCOTICS, AND OTHER BAD STUFF

An elite group of the U.S. Navy, SEAL Team 6, climbed aboard two modified Black Hawk helicopters in 2011. Their mission, two years in the planning, was to capture Osama bin Laden, the founder of the terrorist organization Al-Qaeda.

The helicopters set off for Pakistan under the cover of darkness. Alongside the team was a combat assault canine named Cairo. The Belgian Malinois was highly trained to sniff out and identify explosives and track enemy fighters. In such an important mission, the nose of a dog was indispensable.

← Goggles protect a war dog's eyes from the blinding sun of Southwest Asia. Zorro is a military working dog for the 379th Expeditionary Security Forces Squadron. Canine handlers are trained to protect their dogs from harsh conditions and even to supply medical treatment if necessary.

While the president of the United States sat in his briefing room waiting for word from Operation Neptune Spear, Cairo was storming the compound in Pakistan with the SEALs. He and his handler were on the ground searching the perimeter for explosives and for anyone fleeing the scene.

When their successful mission was complete and the team reported the death of Osama bin Laden, Cairo was among the heroes honored for his bravery and skill. Even President Barack Obama wanted to "meet that dog."

Cairo may have taken part in one of the most important missions in the history of our military, but like all dogs and humans serving in the military,

MAJOR RICHARDSON'S WAR DOGS   "WAITING FOR STRETCHER BEARERS"

Two of Major Richardson's English war dogs wait for help on a World War I battlefield.

he followed a long line of heroes. Dogs have been on the front lines of battle since battles have been fought. During the Middle Ages, in fact, dogs went to war in chain mail armor, just like knights and horses.

Germany, England, and France used canines for all sorts of jobs during World War I. Cigarette dogs carried cigarettes to stressed-out soldiers in the field. Ratters cleaned out rodents from the camps. Sentries and patrol dogs assisted the troops in battle, and ambulance dogs transported first-aid supplies to wounded soldiers. Although the United States didn't have an official war dog program, there were thousands of dogs that accompanied soldiers onto the battlefields.

Perhaps the most famous dog, now known as the first United States war dog hero, was Sgt. Stubby. The bull terrier was smuggled into the 102nd Infantry, 26th (Yankee) Division, out of New Haven, Connecticut, by his owner, Private J. Robert Conroy. The little dog became famous for locating fallen U.S. soldiers during seventeen battles. General John J. Pershing recognized the valiant dog with a gold medal in 1921. Sgt. Stubby visited the White House in 1921 to meet President Warren G. Harding and again in 1924 to meet President Calvin Coolidge.

According to a May 1921 *National Geographic Bulletin*, "There were about 10,000 dogs employed at the battle front at the time of the signing of the armistice. They ranged from Alaskan malamute to St. Bernard and from Scotch collie to fox terrier. Many of them are placed on the regimental rosters like soldiers. In the trenches they shared all the perils and hardships of the

PERMISSION

A military dog and its soldier handler are granted leave during World War II.

soldiers, themselves, and drew their turns in the rest camps in the same fashion. But they were always ready to go back, and it is not recorded that a single one ever failed when it came to going 'over the top.'"

And from the same bulletin: "But there was another type of dog worker needed in the trenches—the liaison dog, trained to seek his master whenever turned loose. Amid exploding shells, through veritable fields of hell, he would crawl or creep with only one thought—to reach his master. Nor would he stop until the object of his search was attained."

After World War I there was such outcry from Americans to honor the seven thousand dogs that served during the war that a monument was built at the Hartsdale Pet Cemetery in Westchester County, New York.

Dogs continued to serve in the military after the First World War. There were four hundred and thirty-six scout dogs employed during World

War II. The U.S. Department of Defense claims the dogs could detect enemy soldiers from a thousand yards (914.4 meters) away. During the Korean War fifteen hundred military working dogs served in Korea, mostly on guard duty. The number jumped to four thousand dogs during the Vietnam War.

There are now approximately thirty-two hundred canines serving in our military throughout the world. They sniff out explosives, missing and fallen soldiers, and enemies. About six hundred of them are in the dry deserts of the Middle East. They not only serve with our troops, they also serve in every U.S. embassy. Special explosive detection dogs even protect the president during presidential inaugurations.

Many more detection dogs serve with police, border patrol, and other agencies. These dogs sniff out explosives, illegal drugs, smuggled animals and plants, and even hiding humans.

Staff Sgt. Kristina Baker has her dog Rex search an all-terrain vehicle near an entry gate to Baghdad International Airport during an explosives search in 2003, during Operation Iraqi Freedom. The two were part of the first air force canine teams deployed to Camp Sather at the airport. →

Sgt. Ed O'Flaherty on duty with his sniffer dog Falcone, named for Detective John M. Falcone, who was killed on duty in Poughkeepsie, New York, in 2011.

Like all sniffer working dogs, these canines are well-schooled. All objects produce an odor that dogs can detect. Dogs trained to sniff out explosives are qualified to detect all the different odors in the explosives set, including ammonium nitrate, TNT, smokeless powder, and plastic explosives. The Metropolitan Transportation Authority (MTA) police in New York use the dogs and require them to search in all kinds of circumstances—on subways and trains, in stations, on the street, and in cars.

Unlike most of his fellow MTA police officers, Sgt. Ed O'Flaherty feeds and walks his partner before leaving for work. Of course, his partner is a two-and-a-half-year-old German shepherd named Falcone. "You want to go to work?" he asks. Falcone jumps. He's ready.

Sgt. Ed suits up and they're off. Today they're at the historic Grand Central Terminal in the heart of New York City. Millions of commuters and visitors use the station and its subways—about seven hundred thousand to a million every day. The mission for Sgt. Ed and Falcone is to keep them safe.

The MTA, with upwards of fifty canine teams, K9 for short, has the largest police K9 unit in the country. Even though there were explosive detection dogs in New York City prior to the September 11 attacks, the current MTA K9 unit was established in June of 2002 to boost the city's counterterrorism efforts.

Falcone is Sgt. Ed's second K9 partner. His first K9 partner, eleven-year-old Duke, is now retired and lives at home with Sgt. Ed's family. He watched out the window as Falcone jumped into the white police SUV to go off to work instead of him. "I would see Duke upstairs barking at the window when I'd leave with Falcone. I had to finally block him off from the window in the morning so he wouldn't see me leave without him," says Sgt. Ed.

These dogs appear to love their jobs. All the explosive detection dogs (EDDs) on the MTA force have gone through twelve weeks of intensive training. That's five days a week, forty hours each week. The dogs are paired up with officers during the training, but might not end up with the same officer by the end.

"Throughout the first month, we might switch dogs three or four times to find a good fit," says Sgt. Ed. Sometimes a calm officer might be paired with a more hyper dog to balance the team. The trainers observe the dogs and the officers throughout training to make sure the right fit is made. Once an officer and a dog are paired, the officer will usually keep the dog for the rest of its life.

Can you imagine training your dog for 360 hours? It's pretty rare to see these dogs make a mistake after they have finished training. A dog's nose just knows.

Throughout the hours of training, the dogs learn to alert their handler when they sniff any type of explosive component. They are trained using towels laced with the scents of different explosives. When the dog locates the scent and alerts correctly, it is rewarded with a game of tug with its handler. Like all training, there is a lot of repetition.

Once trained, the dogs are able to alert their handler to the subtle smells

↑ Falcone and Sgt. Ed in Grand Central Terminal.

of black powder left in a bag that once held a gun. They also alert to the much bigger scent of a truck loaded with legal explosives used in city construction projects. They remain on-lead and close to their handler during their search.

When an EDD locates an explosive it is trained to sit, stay calm, look straight ahead, and wait for its reward. This is called a passive alert and is unnatural for a dog. The natural behavior for a dog when it finds something of interest is to bite, scratch, or bark. Therefore, dogs trained in finding narcotics with police can be trained in a much shorter time because their alert doesn't have to be so restrained—and there are only six odors to identify. These dogs are not finding something that can be deadly upon impact.

Rocky, a sable German shepherd clad in a police vest, is one of those dogs. He is trained to detect marijuana and a variety of narcotics, including cocaine and methamphetamines. Today he lies at the feet of Officer Don Jones at a suburban mall. Curious shoppers stop by to say hello and ask to pet the ninety-five-pound canine. The dog seems relaxed but on closer inspection, you can see the dog's ears are peaked and alert.

Officer Don of the Guilderland, New York, police department has worked with his narcotics detection dog since 2007. Dr. David Wolfe of Shaker Veterinary donated the canine to the department

Like the EDDs, Rocky sniffs the grille, wheel wells, and door seams of a car in search of narcotics. Unlike the EDDs, if he locates something, he will aggressively scratch at the car and bark his alert. ↓

after the death of the department's previous K9, Niko. Students in the Guilderland Animal Protection Society at the Farnsworth Middle School named the dog Rocky.

Rocky: Five-and-a-half-year-old German shepherd, on patrol and narcotics detection since 2007.

Rocky is trained to respond only to Officer Don's German commands. Upon hearing the language, Rocky is all work and no play. Although he can play tug and fetch until he drops, the K9 is cross-trained to detect narcotics and to work patrol with Officer Don.

Rocky has been involved in hundreds of drug arrests since he joined the force in 2007, including sniffing out eight pounds of marijuana hidden in the trunk of a car. Officer Don and Rocky check local schools and also assist other communities with their investigations.

The U.S. Transportation Security Agency, Federal Aviation Administration, FBI, and U.S. Customs officials all depend on dogs to locate an ever-increasing selection of illegal narcotics quickly and, unlike humans, do so without bias. They are searching purely for scent. It makes no difference to the dogs who might be carrying it.

According to Sgt. Ed, it is rare to see a police department dog trained in both narcotics and explosives. "They are two completely different things with different odors and different alerts. You wouldn't want to see a dog sit and alert, and wonder if there is a pound of cocaine behind a cabinet or ten pounds of TNT. If it's explosives, you want to get the bomb squad in and the whole area is getting shut down."

There are many traits that make a super explosive detection dog. "We want a dog that is driven and has a lot of play drive," says Sgt. Ed. The sociability is also important, especially in the environment of the MTA canines. "We've got people around here all day, with elderly and children." These dogs have to be friendly around a lot of people.

The MTA canines also have to be able to work in an environment with loud train whistles, fire truck honks, scaffolding, and stairs. "You can have a really tough dog in the country, but you take him in front of a diesel train and he could shut down," says Sgt. Ed. That sometimes separates usable dogs from unusable dogs. The MTA training facility is in the country, away from the loud city noises. During training the dogs are brought into the city to make sure they can work in both settings.

They also work in some extreme conditions. "The tunnels can reach a hundred and twenty degrees," says MTA officer Greg Rozsay. "You try to limit their exposure."

"We can be down there awhile if we are looking for someone or we have a specific threat," says Sgt. Ed.

The dogs can become stressed during long work periods in extreme conditions. The handlers have to recognize the signs of distress because the dogs

Seren, named for the Welsh word for "star," and Officer Greg on patrol in a tunnel of Grand Central Terminal.

YOU USE YOUR EYES. SHE'LL USE HER NOSE.

We're counting on everyone.
Tell a cop, an MTA employee, or call 1-888-NYC-SAFE.

IF YOU SEE SOMETHING, SAY SOMETHING.

Metropolitan
Transportation
Authority

↑ This explosive detection dog, Emmy, is the poster dog for the MTA K9 program.

won't quit. They need to take a break when the dogs start panting, yawning, or jumping around. Handlers can take their dogs into their temperature-controlled vehicles or into the station office for some downtime before heading out again.

The dogs are certified by the New York State Department of Criminal Justice every year for explosive detection, but many are also certified every two years to be patrol dogs. The teams also have training days every month to keep them sharp and reinforce skills. Like other working dogs, EDDs are in great shape. Sgt. Ed says, "A dog searching for ten minutes is like a man running fast for an hour." They always have to be prepared to work at that level. Have you heard the expression "worked like a dog"? Well, these dogs really do work hard.

Sometimes the dogs have the opportunity to sniff out large quantities of explosives. Explosives companies will give the MTA and local law enforcement a heads up when they are transporting explosives and let the canines come out to test with much larger amounts. You might be surprised to learn that the dogs provide the same professional restrained alert. Sometimes the officers will put out an ounce of an explosive and then put out twenty pounds to give the dogs the opportunity to test their skills. It provides the canines with a great teaching tool.

"I have the best job," says Officer Greg, laughing. "I get to walk my dog all day." Of course, there is much more to his job, but these officers love and trust their dogs immensely. "I was al-

Falcone: two-and-a-half-year-old German shepherd on the job detecting explosives in New York City.

ways a dog lover," says Officer Greg. "I grew up having dogs."

"Any time I saw a K9 cop I always thought it was the coolest thing. I always wanted to work a dog. I love dogs and I love being a cop. It's the perfect match," says Sgt. Ed. He agrees that canines make great partners. "All they want to do is play and love you."

Officer Greg's partner is one-and-a-half-year-old Seren, his third dog since he joined the unit. Both Seren and Falcone came from the Jersey Seeing Eye Club. Seren's name comes from a woman from the Seeing Eye Club who found many dogs for the MTA. Being of Welsh background, she named the dog Seren, Welsh for "star." Officer Greg kept the name. With their high play drive and active temperament, Falcone and Seren were not cut out to be Seeing Eye dogs. But thanks to the Seeing Eye trainers, they have found a challenging and rewarding second career.

Falcone and Seren are trained to sniff all kinds of different objects for explosives. They can sweep through a line of cars outside the station if a threat has been made, or their handler might have them sniff a package left beside a commuter train.

Other detection dogs are trained to walk through a crowd of people and sniff the air for the molecules of explosive particles lingering in the air. Unlike Falcone and Seren, these explosive detection canines are trained to pick up the scent on moving people.

Auburn University boasts a premier training program for this type of

explosive detection, known as vapor wake detection. Vapor wake dogs have been called a four-legged antiterror tool. Like many of these sniffing canines, they come with a hefty price tag of $20,000 each. These dogs are amazingly talented, but the problem lies in the minutes or seconds after the dog alerts. If the dog is in a crowded area and the suspect carrying the explosive is discovered, protocols need to be in place to ensure the safety of the dog and the surrounding people, who are instantly in danger.

Other dogs are trained as accelerant detection dogs (ADDs). They assist fire investigators by sniffing out traces of petroleum products such as gasoline or lighter fluid that might have been used to deliberately start a fire. Hundreds of lives are lost each year from intentionally set fires, or arson. The traces of accelerants found by the dogs are sampled and sent to a lab for identification to help investigators with their analysis and prosecution.

Braith, whose name is Gaelic for "detect," sniffs out an accelerant during training.

You might have heard these dogs called "arson dogs," but that is an outdated and incorrect term. According to the Canine Accelerant Detection Association, these dogs cannot detect whether a fire was accidentally set or was arson. They can only detect the presence of accelerants. It is up to fire investigators to take that information and determine the cause of a fire.

To become certified for the work, the dogs and their handlers undergo three hundred hours of professional training that not only incorporates accelerant identification, but also familiarizes the dogs with helicopters and other modes of transportation they might use. Handlers are also instructed to care for their dogs and learn how to collect samples at the scene of a fire. Accelerant detection teams must pass yearly tests to maintain their certification. In the end, they are single-purpose, single-handler dogs. They are not trained for any other types of detection work and will be with only one handler during their career.

Like EDDs, these dogs are trained to give a passive alert. Even though the accelerants are not dangerous, they are evidence that needs to be protected from damage. According to deputy

Handlers use samples of accelerants during training with their dogs. ↓

chief of the New York State Arson Bureau Randi Shadic, any disturbance by the dogs would further compromise the accelerant evidence after the fire.

Ashes: four-year-old black Labrador, shelter rescue, on the job since 2010.

"These dogs have a high play drive and a high hunt drive, which is critical to their ability to learn and apply their skills," says Chief Randi, who had his own accelerant detection dog for ten years. He describes the training process as "chaining." "Each step in the process is another link in the chain, resulting in the canine being able to search, locate, and indicate the finding of trace ignitable liquid." Chief Randi and his dog, Mica, logged thousands of searches as a team.

Accelerant detection dogs are pretty new to the working dog roster. The Atlantic City Police Department was one of the first agencies to begin training and using them in the 1980s. In 1988 the New York State Office of Fire Prevention and Control (OFPC) sent two fire investigators to be trained as handlers in New Jersey. Once trained, they worked for the next five years with their Labrador partners, K9 Buddy and K9 Hershey.

In 1993 the intensive three-hundred-hour training program was established in New York State. Over the years, the New York OFPC Arson Unit

Ashes exhibiting a passive sitting alert during training.

has had nine K9 teams among their ranks and has trained many more. State Farm Insurance also began its extensive accelerant alert dog program in 1993. The company now has more than three hundred dogs working in forty-four states, Washington, D.C., and Canada.

↑ Braith once got sprayed in the face by a skunk and still went to work at eight the next morning. There's no stopping these dogs!

Many of the Labrador retrievers used by the OFPC are rescue dogs or dogs finding their niche after being unsuccessful Seeing Eye dogs. "We are reclaiming these dogs to give them a new purpose," says Chief Randi.

Like the explosive detection dogs and narcotics detection dogs working for police and fire companies, the ADDs are able to retire and live out their days with their handler after their working career is over. This was not always the case with the dogs working in the military.

Until recently all war dogs were officially still considered "surplus equipment," which prohibited the military from paying for their return to the United States. In fact, only a handful of the nearly five thousand dogs that served in the military in Vietnam returned to the United States. Over twenty-five hundred were left behind to inexperienced handlers in the South Vietnamese army and another sixteen hundred were euthanized. President Bill Clinton signed a law in 2000 that allowed military dogs to be adopted. Cairo's publicity has helped to bring attention to these dogs. Americans are becoming more aware of the services these dogs accomplish for our military. They save lives, and they've experienced everything a two-footed member of the military does: gunshots, combat, and heavy training. They deserve a peaceful retirement.

Unlike some of the other detection dogs, military EDDs do not always have one handler. Many times they pass from handler to handler, soldier to soldier. Eventually the dog reaches the point of retirement.

Cairo is inspiring a record num-

Braith: seven-year-old chocolate Labrador, detecting accelerants since 2007.

ber of adoptions of these dogs, helping these amazing animals achieve the peace they deserve back in the States. Applications for their adoptions have increased, even though it can cost upwards of $2,000 to bring them home.

Ron Aiello, president of the U.S. War Dogs Association, believes Cairo's story is helping change the current military policy, classifying these dogs as "canine veterans" instead of "military surplus" and making the military responsible for bringing them home to adoptive families or previous handlers.

Senior Airman Stephen Hanks, a 447th Expeditionary Security Forces Squadron military working dog handler, and Geri, a three-year-old patrol explosive detection dog, take a break after a hard day of training at their kennel in Baghdad, Iraq, on December 9, 2011. Stephen and Geri are deployed from Patrick Air Force Base, Florida. ↙

Inmates at seven prisons in New York State are taking part in a unique training program. They receive eight-week-old puppies and spend their days training them to become EDDs and other types of service dogs. The dogs live in the cell with their trainers and receive careful, dedicated instruction. "It's not easy. It's a twenty-four-hour-a-day job," says Jan Brady, a Puppies Behind Bars instructor.

This program is a new "leash" on life not only for these dogs, who will become hard-working members of our society, but also for the inmates themselves. For some prisoners, these dogs are their first experience with unconditional love. Others haven't had the opportunity to pet a dog in years.

In August of 2012 a new group of puppies graduated from the Puppies Behind Bars program. A black Labrador named Colton was among them, sitting proudly with his new handler, a U.S. Marine. Colton was named after LCpl. Colton Rusk, who lost his life in Afghanistan. He left behind his beloved explosive detection dog, Eli, who was adopted by his family. Fundraising efforts on Colton Rusk's behalf enabled the young Labrador to be trained to be a service dog for a wounded veteran.

ECO SNIFFERS

Meet Tucker, a black brindled Labrador retriever mix with an extremely cool job. Tucker is a conservation detection dog, or eco dog. He works on land and on sea. He's trained to track the scat of wolverines, gray wolves, moose, caribou, and orca whales.

Scat, a polite scientific word for an animal's poop, can provide a lot of clues about animal populations. By examining a scat sample, scientists can find out what the animal ate. They can also determine its food habits, parasites, habitat use, and the abundance of the species. Further scientific tests on DNA found within a scat sample can help conservationists determine the sex, species, paternity, and range, and even identify the individual animal that left the scat behind. These studies are crucial when conservationists are looking at changes in animal population that might be affected by disease, habitat loss, or diet changes.

Tucker is one of the many working dogs that have joined the ranks of the nation's most intrepid conservationists. Eco dogs locate everything from moose scat in the Adirondack Mountains to invasive snails in Hawaii, desert tortoises in Nevada, brown tree snakes in Guam, tigers in Cambodia, and cheetahs in Kenya. Their skilled tracking yields lots of information for scientists.

Even though their job is very important, these dogs don't start out being anything special. In fact, most eco dogs, like many live-find dogs, are adopted from animal shelters. According to biologist Alice Whitelaw of Working Dogs for Conservation, the best conservation dogs are those that are "bouncing off the walls" at a shelter and so toy-obsessed they refuse to put down their toy no matter what. These energetic misfits might not turn out to be good family lap dogs, but they are superb eco dogs.

Heath Smith, program coordinator for the Conservation Canines (CK-9) of the University of Washington's Center for Conservation Biology, agrees. Their high energy and overfocused behavior are a perfect mix of traits for a dog that will be out on the trail with conservation scientists for four to six hours at a time.

Once a dog is identified as a potential eco dog, the trainer begins the training process by playing with a ball. The ball will eventually become a reward for finding the object of its search.

"It takes the dogs five minutes to get used to the ball," Heath says. "Then about a month to teach them to search and alert. Lots of repetition."

Heath continues: "What is fantastic about the dogs is that they don't care about anything else but getting their ball. If the scat is floating in the water or up on a volcanic rock or in a gully of boulders, the dogs work their best to either reach it or point it out to their handlers. The real treasure is the communication that takes place between the handler and their dog. That communication is a special bond."

All handlers agree that they rely on their dogs for their data. They wouldn't get it if it weren't for their dogs.

↑ Tucker has picked up the scent of whale scat and alerts his handler, Heath.

Tucker, dressed in a bright yellow vest, jumps into the boat with his handler. Even though he doesn't like to swim, he hops up to the bow, ready for today's search game. The boat motors off and Tucker, his nose to the wind, begins searching out the scent of orca scat. It's tough. Orca scat, unlike bright orange right whale scat that's easily seen in the water, is slimy, resembles the seawater, and sinks quickly. That doesn't deter Tucker, because he's not relying on his eyes. He's sniffing it out. As soon as his nose catches a whiff of the scat, he's ready to pull his handler overboard to get to it. Tucker has no interest in the actual whales, but has been trained to know that if he locates orca feces, he gets to play ball.

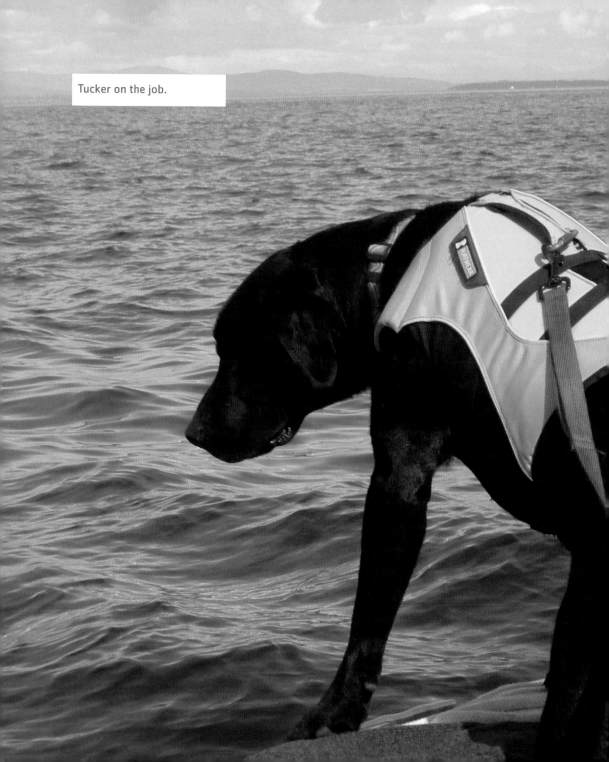

Tucker on the job.

Dogs and whales? They couldn't be more different, and yet Tucker isn't the only conservation dog being employed to save one of the world's endangered whales. Fargo, a rottweiler, and a mutt named Bob helped scientists from the New England Aquarium locate the bright orange right whale feces in the Atlantic Ocean for further study.

Fargo, with his head down and low on the bow of the boat, was able to locate the scat of a right whale up to one nautical mile away. Bob, with his snout to the air, found the scent from even farther away.

By locating and collecting the scat, scientists are able to study the population of the endangered whales in an effort to protect the remaining individuals. In the case that Tucker was helping to investigate, scientists were looking at why the population of killer whales found between Washington State and Alaska was declining. They had three ideas, or hypotheses. The first involved the decline of the whales' prey, the Chinook salmon. Perhaps there just wasn't enough food for them in those waters. The second involved the disturbance of the whales' habitat by commercial and private whale watchers that might have been frightening off the population. Scientists also feared that toxins in the water were collecting in the fat of the whales and making them sick. Just one of

Tucker: black brindled Labrador retriever mix professional on land or at sea.

those factors, or a combination of them, might be causing the decline of the whales. Studying the whales' scat enabled scientists to examine all of these ideas. It also enabled scientists to develop the first pregnancy test for wild baleen whales by measuring the hormone levels in the scat they collected.

Tucker and the other eco dogs that track whales weren't initially trained in the water to locate the scat. They began their training on land, like all other eco dogs. Trainers position scat in containers for the dogs to find. Once they do, they are rewarded with a game.

After Tucker learned the smell of the scat on land, Heath then floated samples of scat in Tupperware containers in the inlets of Puget Sound for him to locate. According to Heath, the real challenge in locating whale scat with an eco dog is steering the boat. "It's hard to keep up with where the dogs want to go."

Wicket is another eco dog who had her beginnings at an animal shelter and has become one of the best. This black Labrador mix, who went by the name of Cooper at the Pintler Pets Animal Shelter in Montana, was overactive and would rile up the other dogs. Her obsessive behavior made her unadoptable.

"And here she was just a stray. No one wanted her," said the shelter's Pat Phillips. In fact, when Alice Whitelaw arrived from Working Dogs for Conservation (WDC), Pat said, "Oh, you don't want her, she's crazy."

That wild behavior was just what WDC was looking for. After just one interview they "hired" Wicket. They knew she would make a terrific eco dog.

And they were right. She was able to get to work after only nine weeks of training and made her handlers proud by sniffing out fifty-two scats in a single day. A photo of Wicket on assignment in Guam now hangs proudly in the lobby of the animal shelter. Wicket was wicked good!

"It warms your heart to think that they were throwaways, and now look at them. The dogs are happy because they are doing a job," says Pat. "It's great that they [the WDC] look to shelters to find dogs."

Wicket, a black Lab mix, is a world-traveling veteran eco dog. ↓

A moose's daily munching can alter a landscape.

Wicket was one of two eco dogs that took part in the appropriately named AROMA (Adirondack Return of Moose Assessment) project in New York's Adirondack Park. The Wildlife Conservation Society (WCS) teamed up with Working Dogs for Conservation in 2008.

The traditional way for scientists to study a local moose population is to use helicopters, tranquilizers, and radio collars. According to Heidi Kretser, a WCS scientist, "it's invasive, very hard, and very expensive."

The moose population had vanished by the early 1860s due to rampant hunting and the growth of agriculture in the Adirondacks. With the onset of regulated hunting and land management, in the 1980s the moose began a natural migration from neighboring regions back to the park. Their population has been of intense interest ever since.

The New York State Department of Environmental Conservation believes that there are now between eight hundred and a thousand moose in the park; however, there are no scientific reports to validate that estimate.

Scientists need to know how these huge moose will impact the environment as they return to the park. These 500- to 1,200-pound (227–544 kilograms) mammals can change whole landscapes as they trample and graze through the park, looking for dinner.

In spring, summer, and fall, a moose can eat forty to sixty pounds of food each day, depending on the animal's size. They eat everything from tall grasses and catkins to woody plants. Scientists need an update on the growing population so they can manage the park in the future.

But doing a traditional study was not possible, due to the cost and logistics of covering such a large area. At over nine thousand square miles, the park is 2.75 times larger than Yellowstone National Park. "Considering that the Adirondack Park is six million acres, there was absolutely no way we could conceivably try to start a functional [tracking] project for the amount of money it would cost to have all the logistics on the ground," said Heidi.

Eco dogs, however, are less expensive and less harmful to the environment. Wicket and her conservation dog buddies can locate moose scat for scientists to analyze instead of using difficult traditional tracking practices performed by people.

"WCS had been using the dogs for a project out west, collecting carnivore scat from lions, wolves, and bears. They had had great success with them," said Heidi. "There was no reason to not try them."

After securing the funding and planning for a solid year, WCS invited Working Dogs for Conservation to come to the Adirondacks for the study.

Wicket is an air-scent dog. Her nose is not to the ground to track the moose. She sniffs the air for a whiff of moose scat. For Wicket to learn how to locate Adirondack moose scat, Heidi had to send a sample out to Montana. It was important to have the

Wicket: rescued black Labrador mix, world traveling conservation canine.

Wicket leading the way during Project AROMA.

actual scat to reflect the Adirondack environment where the moose live. Like all scat, it would emit the odor of what the animal ate. Adirondack moose eat the plants that grow in the park. Montana moose scat would have a different scent.

Aimee Hurt, cofounder and associate director of Working Dogs for Conservation, set out a group of scent boxes back in Montana for Wicket. One contained the pellets of moose scat and a hole for the scent to release. Moose scat resembles deer scat, but the oval pellets are slightly larger.

Wicket could see the boxes. When she located the box with the scent, Aimee threw the toy. After some repetitions Wicket eventually associated that smell with play. Aimee moved the scent box farther away, out of sight. She continued the process until Wicket learned to locate the scent and sit to alert her handler when she found it. She was then ready for the North Country woods of the Adirondack Mountains.

Wicket arrived with Aimee, Camas, and Camas's handler, Alice Whitelaw. "It was a little bit of a dice game," said Heidi. The scats the dogs had trained on were from the fall, and it was now spring. Scats vary from season to season, depending on the vegetation the moose are eating. Even though the scats Wicket and Camas were now looking for had a slightly different scent, the two dogs were able to identify them.

Without the help of previous studies, Heidi and her team had to rely on word-of-mouth moose sightings to plan and map out the grid for the dogs' visit. They used maps, GPS, and a compass to record where they were and where they had located scat.

According to Working Dogs for Conservation, air-scent dogs don't see a landscape of mountains, valleys, trees, and grass like we do. They see a "scent-scape" full of all the different smells of the area. The dogs were previously trained to locate bear scat, so the handlers collected black bear scat in the field

Camas: on the job in the Adirondacks.

as well. "We found one hundred and forty-one moose scats," said Heidi, proudly.

The scats were packed up and sent to the Rocky Mountain Research Station for further laboratory study. Unfortunately, it took time to acquire enough funds to begin the testing involved on the numerous scats collected. "We didn't know we'd be so successful," said Heidi.

The scientists also needed tissue samples from individual moose to compare to the scat they found. With the tissue samples and the scat, the scientists could then determine how closely related the moose in the Adirondacks were to moose in neighboring states. They were able to obtain thirty-eight tissue samples from the New York State Department of Environmental Conservation and from neighboring states. From those samples, they were able to identify twenty-five individual Adirondack moose. Some of the moose scat samples collected were generated from the same moose that had traveled from area to area.

Wicket and Camas helped WCS determine that the Adirondack moose population is very similar to those in Vermont, New Hampshire, and Maine and in Quebec and Ontario south of the St. Lawrence River, but not north of it. Although there is still more to be learned, the conservation dogs assisted in securing vital data for the scientists. The dogs' noses proved they could be another tool in a scientist's kit. WCS is hoping to have the eco dogs back to the park in the future to continue the study.

Wicket, now a pro in finding moose scat, is working on a new project

Camas locates scat.

A U.S. Customs and Border Protection Beagle Brigade looks for prohibited agricultural products.

in Wyoming. Teams are out in the field searching for Shiras moose scat for scientists from the University of Wyoming and the Wyoming Cooperative Fish and Wildlife Unit. The Shiras moose are a small subspecies named for George Shiras III, a politician, conservationist, and photographer from Pennsylvania. The moose are thriving in some parts of the state, but not in others. The moose scat study will help the scientists find out why.

Wicket, Tucker, and the rest of the working eco dogs do more than hunt scat and help with population studies. Their job description widens with each project. Scientists all over the world are finding out that conservation dogs can locate just about anything they are asked to.

The famous "Beagle Brigade" is a familiar sight at twenty-one international airports in the United States. But don't confuse these airport sniffing dogs with their explosive-detecting officemates. The beagles, known for their strong sniffing skills, are the first line of defense used by the U.S. Department of Agriculture (USDA) and the U.S. Customs and Border Protection against alien wildlife species that could harm our environment.

The dogs don't just find the sandwich stashed in your bag; they find small insects that might be hiding on a piece of fruit you've packed, or the smuggled illegal bushmeat from Africa and Asia. They can also sniff out the nasty insect, brought deliberately to the United States by bioterrorists, that could wreak havoc with our agriculture.

Unlike most other working dogs, the USDA beagles do not work for play. They work for a food reward. When they detect prohibited fruits, vegetables, and meats in someone's baggage, the beagles are trained to sit and give a passive alert to their handler. The handler rewards the dog with a bite of food instead of a ball.

These special types of conservation detection dogs are not limited to the United States. In Ecuador, dogs search boats returning from the Galápagos Islands with smuggled illegal shark fins or other illegal wildlife and contraband.

Asia added its first working canine to its customs staff with the help of the animal welfare organization Animals Asia. The organization's detective dog, Simba, began work in 2000 at Incheon Airport in South Korea. The golden Labrador retriever sniffed out illegal wildlife products, such as ivory, snakes, baby monkeys, and bear gallbladders, which were being smuggled into the country. In recognition of his success, Simba was awarded an honorary certificate for his "exceptional service" by the South Korean minister of the environment. In a part of the world where dogs are considered by some to be both pets and food, this was a huge leap. Unfortunately, because the authorities didn't make many arrests even when Simba did detect illegal items, it became necessary to retire the dog. Perhaps one day they will be willing to try the program again.

New Zealand's Department of Conservation has its own National Conservation Dog Programme, employing detection dogs. Since 1890, New Zealand has been using dogs to help protect the country's wildlife. The department now employs two types of detection dogs—protected species de-

tection dogs (PSDDs) and predator detection dogs (PDDs). Officials use PSDDs to give a passive alert when they detect certain target species that are under population studies, such as kiwi birds, geckos, and even wood roses. PDDs search for rats, cats,

and other introduced predators that are harmful to the environment.

Introduced and alien species are a problem throughout the world. Some are deliberately brought and others arrive by accident. The tiny rosy wolf-snail looks harmless, but has done decades of damage to the environment in Hawaii. Can eco dogs sniff them out? Of course.

A mix of light rain and snow fell on a Montana forest. Wicket, clad in a bright orange vest, was all business with her nose in the air. The weather

Can you tell the difference between species of purple lupine flowers? Probably not. But Rogue, a Belgian sheepdog, can. Not all lupines are equal. Only one species plays host to a rare butterfly. Kincaid's lupine flowers are crucial to the survival of the rare Fender's blue butterfly. Rogue, trained by Dave Vesely, an ecologist at the Oregon Wildlife Institute, can tell the difference between species even when his scientist handlers can't.

"There's nothing more fun than being out working with these dogs in the morning, when the birds are singing, and you know you're doing good conservation work," says Dave. "I just love it."

didn't bother her at all. Her job during this new training was to locate a well-camouflaged light brown snail the size of a thumb that had been positioned for her to locate. Eventually she picked up the scent, sat up, and locked eyes with her teammate, Aimee Hurt. Aimee quickly rewarded Wicket with a toss of a ball from her belt pack. The dog ran off to fetch it.

Wicket was training to locate this invasive species. It was brought to the Hawaiian Islands in 1955 to attack the troublesome giant African snail, but, like other alien species, it moved on and found other things to eat. It is now listed as one of the world's one hundred worst invaders. The team headed off for the island of Oahu after it completed five to six hundred of these practice sessions in Montana.

Wicket and Aimee flew to Hawaii with two other dogs, Tia and Tsavo, and their handler, Alice Whitelaw. Far away from the surfboards on Waikiki Beach, the Waianae Mountains rise in a jagged green line across Oahu, much different from the cool woods the dogs were used to. It's here that the U.S. Army is fighting an unlikely battle to protect the tiny Oahu tree snail from the cannibal rosy wolfsnail. Working Dogs for Conservation was there to help fight the battle with the Oahu Army Natural Resource Program (OANRP).

"The army, as a federal agency, is required to protect threatened and endangered species found on its installations," said Kapua Kawelo, OANRP biologist, U.S. Army Garrison–Hawaii. "On Oahu, the army is required to stabilize the population of the endangered Oahu tree snail in eight locations

Tsavo: career-changed German shepherd, now living a life of leisure post-retirement.

across the Waianae Mountains; each location includes around three hundred snails per population."

It seems a lot of work to save a tiny snail, but the Oahu tree snails are special. First of all, they aren't found anywhere else in the entire world! Living in such a rugged mountain range caused the snails to become isolated into different groups. They evolved into different species, each with a beautiful patterned shell. There used to be forty-one different tree snails in Oahu, but now there are only six or seven different snails, and all but two of those are endangered. And that is just the beginning of why they need protection.

Pristine forests, like the ones in the mountains of Oahu, recharge and maintain our water systems, according to conservation geneticist Dr. Brenden Holland of the University of Hawaii. When the forest ecosystem becomes disturbed, our water systems suffer. The decline of the tree snail population tells us that the forest is in trouble. Scientists call it an indicator species. When it is in trouble, the forest is in trouble. Studying the snails helps the whole forest ecosystem.

Wicket, Tia, and Tsavo handled the long flight from Montana well, but they were itching to get out of their crates. Not yet! First the dogs needed to be quarantined and papers filled out. Officials had to make sure the dogs were free from ticks, fleas, or anything else they might bring to the islands. It was important that the dogs didn't bring in any alien species on their mission to help locate another. Once the dogs were cleared, Aimee and Alice allowed them to leave their crates and stretch their legs.

The scents on the island were a lot different from those in Montana. Before they could get to work, the dogs needed to get acclimated to all these new smells and warm temperatures. The dogs and their handlers spent a couple of days getting used to their rental house on Oahu's North Shore, eat-

A bit of relaxing for the eco dogs after their long flight to Hawaii. ↘

ing normal dinners and just shaking off the long flight. The dogs had some short training sessions, no longer than about twenty minutes each. They smelled the snails and got used to locating them in these new conditions. Then real training in the mountains began.

Data was collected. Aimee and Alice proceeded slowly. The dogs dealt with heavy moisture and thick leaf litter in the Waianae Mountains. The snails emitted very little scent. It's a tough job for human biologists and dogs, even professionals like Wicket, Tsavo, and Tia. Aimee likened it to the difficulty of "finding a single drop of blood at a busy crime scene," but Wicket and her team of eco dogs did it.

The handlers were down on all fours helping the dogs find the scent. They crawled along, searching for the tiny snails. The team spent roughly four hours each day working in the field. The dogs rested up for their next trip into the field whenever they had some downtime. Although difficult, the trip was successful, with the dogs locating the same number of snails as the biologist observers. However, the handlers knew there was potential for the dogs to accomplish even more.

A year later, Aimee and Alice headed back to Hawaii with Wicket and Tia.

Tia: born to be a conservation canine; on the job at Working Dogs for Conservation with Tsavo and Wicket.

Tia finds a snail!

They were right. On this second trip the dogs located snails faster than the humans, and found smaller snails that the biologists frequently missed.

The dogs had proven again that there was no limit to what they could find. Whether it's scat, snails, or a sandwich, these dogs are eager for their next challenge. And who knows what that will be?

MEDICAL SNIFFERS

Zack gets up in the morning, pricks his finger, and checks the level of his blood sugar. He's one of thousands of kids living with type 1, or juvenile, diabetes.

Diabetes is a lifelong disease. When the pancreas has trouble producing the chemical insulin, the body has difficulty moving blood sugar into cells. The sugar builds up and causes many different symptoms. Diabetics often feel very thirsty and very tired. They might get headaches. And they might lose weight without going on a diet. That's what happened to Zack. He had lost sixty pounds and was having trouble fitting into his football uniform when he was diagnosed three years ago.

Like all diabetics, fourteen-year-old Zack adapted his lifestyle to pricking his finger up to twenty times a day and using insulin injections to keep his blood sugar levels regulated. His normal blood sugar level should be between 110 and 180, but at its highest it was reaching 2,000 and at its lowest, 28.

Nighttime is the most dangerous time of day. Because sugar levels can spike during the night and go unnoticed, Zack's mom did nightly two a.m. checks to make sure her son was okay while he slept.

↑ Alan's first day on the job.

For many kids living with this condition, it might mean homeschooling, no playdates, or anything else that will protect them from being at risk during a drastic change in their blood sugar levels. High and low spikes can lead to two very dangerous conditions—a diabetic coma or diabetic ketoacidosis. For Zack it meant he often had trouble attending a full day at school. He'd arrive at school, then halfway through the day his blood sugar level would drop so low that he couldn't continue.

But that was before Alan, a fox red Labrador puppy and trained diabetes alert dog, or DAD, arrived to live with Zack the summer before he entered high school.

Your dog probably sniffs you up, down, and everywhere as soon as you walk into the house. By that one sniff your dog can tell where you've been and what you've been doing. It might surprise you, but your dog probably knows more about your health than you do. Now doctors and families are finding out that a dog's sniffer might just be one of their best diagnostic tools. And even though *your* dog seems like the best sniffer around, these sniffing dogs are specially trained.

Diabetes alert dogs such as Alan are kept in foster homes for training from birth until they are given to a diabetic. That loving environment helps train them to life as a DAD. A scent recognition test is given when they are forty-nine days old, along with personality and temperament tests. They are then entered into an obedience course. The puppies are placed with diabetic families when they are between ten and twelve weeks old.

"It's the quality of life that these dogs give these kids. It's unbelievable," says trainer Dee Bogetti. "It's all about the nose. We pick the best noses out of our litters to become DADs. Then they are trained initially to recognize changes in blood sugar. Once they recognize the scent we train them to alert. Once a DAD is trained 100 percent to her job, she is never wrong."

What does this mean for Zack? "I missed a lot of school. My sugar would drop during the day. Now I won't have to leave," says Zack. Zack's DAD will change everything in his life.

For kids living with this disease, a dog can accompany them when they go away to

Alan: alerts with a gentle mouth that Zack's blood sugar is changing.

college. A DAD can be with them during a sleepover and be their guardian through the night. Or be with them while they take their driver's test, and later alert them before their blood sugar drops too low to drive. A DAD can allow them to run and play and alert them when they need to slow down and test.

Zack's DAD, Alan, comes with a trainer who will visit Zack's family every three months for the first two years. At the end of Alan's training, the dog will be able to alert Zack to a change in his blood sugar level twenty minutes before it happens. He'll tap Zack's knee if his blood sugar is falling or his shoulder if it's rising. If Zack is playing basketball away from Alan or is asleep, the dog will alert Zack's mom. Eventually, Alan will even be able to call 911 on a special phone if Zack has a serious problem and is unresponsive.

These dogs are trained to recognize the sweet smell of high blood sugar levels and the subtle sour smell of low blood sugar levels in the breath of people with diabetes. Alan started his job off right. Upon meeting Zack, the squiggly puppy ran right up to him and alerted him that his blood sugar was high. And he kept on working.

Just over a month after arriving, Alan alerted that Zack's blood sugar had dropped from 3.2 miles (5.1 kilometers) away! That's right, over three miles (5 kilometers) away. Zack was at a football game when Alan started pawing Zack's mom. When she didn't respond, Alan nipped and ran anxious circles until she did. Diabetes alert dogs have been known to scent up to five miles away, but generally the dogs have to be within a thousand yards, or about ten football fields, to accurately alert. The outside conditions, in-

Alan heads into the school for basketball practice with Zack.

cluding wind direction, must have been just right for Alan to alert from so far.

It's October. Alan, taller, tail wagging, runs up the steps after school as Zack heads to basketball practice. Since Alan can't sit on the court as Zack plays, he sits in the stands with Zack's mom. Even high above the players Alan sniffs Zack's blood sugar levels. He sits at Zack's mom's feet until he detects a change; when he does, he gets up and begins alerting. Tug on a leash. Nibble on a hand.

Alan is still in training. He will keep alerting until Zack's level is within a safe range again. That could be a long while. It's no wonder he's nibbled his way through a few leashes in just the first couple of months. Eventually, he'll learn to recognize when his message has been received and it's time to stop alerting.

DADs aren't the only dogs scenting their way into the medical books. Shannon is a young woman with a rare condition that causes her blood pressure to drop suddenly. At her worst she was fainting daily, causing her to suffer numerous concussions. Enter a two-year-old golden Labrador named Clover. Clover gently nudges Shannon when her blood pressure falls and doesn't stop until Shannon sits down. Clover can't prevent her from fainting, but she can keep her safe when she does.

Riley was only five months old when her allergy was diagnosed. Some allergies, such as hay fever, can be annoying, but not life threatening. Others, such as severe peanut allergies, can be deadly. Riley has one of those. Eating peanuts or coming in contact with them is dangerous for her. Even breathing in small particles of peanuts could act like a bomb, causing Riley to go into the very dangerous condition of anaphylaxis.

More and more dogs are being used to help detect dangerous allergens, like peanuts. ↓

Children with severe allergies like Riley's live within a kind of bubble. Their families try their best to keep them safe in a very uncertain world where even a friendly cookie could kill them.

Peanuts or peanut shells are found in everything from candy to potting soil. They might be in an ant trap. Or in a pizza crust. There's no way to know.

"Your world starts to be your house. Even places that had been safe before become unsafe," says Riley's mom, Sherry. As a parent, Sherry searched for a way to give her daughter a normal childhood.

After seeing sniffing beagles at an airport, she asked, "If a dog can find a pineapple, why can't it find a peanut?" She found out—they could.

Riley's life changed when Rock'O entered it. The Portuguese water dog could alert Riley if there were peanuts anywhere or in anything that could hurt her. As an allergy alert dog (AAD), Rock'O was trained to sit when he detected peanuts. When told, "Show me," Rock'O could point with his nose to the offending peanut source.

Rock'O has since passed away and Riley, now twelve, has Cici to help keep her safe. Before an allergy alert dog came into Riley's life, family decisions were based on her disability. Each decision, such as where she would attend school, was based on her safety. These days their alert dog has freed up those decisions. Now whether Riley wants to be homeschooled or attend a public school is her choice. They can be assured she'll be safe in either setting.

Allergy alert dogs are trained to alert for many different allergens, including tree nuts, eggs, soy, dairy, or shellfish. Trainers work with the child's allergist to determine whether a dog can help. Many of the dogs, such as the water dogs and different poodle/retriever mixes, or doodles, are used as

AADs because they are considered allergy-friendly. They shed less and have minimal dander.

There is no end to what alert dogs can detect. Zero, a bio-detection dog, has been trained to detect harmful *E. coli* and salmonella at farms in California before it can make us sick. Other dogs are detecting bedbugs. Still others are finding their way into the medical books. Imagine an early detection system for cancer that doesn't involve an expensive, invasive surgery or a scan.

According to Dr. Suresh S. Ramalingam, associate professor and director of the lung program at Emory University's Winship Cancer Institute in Atlanta, using dogs to detect lung cancer with just a sniff is "the holy grail." It's believed that dogs have the ability to sniff out VOCs (volatile organic compounds). Our breath has about four thousand VOCs. A dog's nose detects tiny changes in these compounds that are sometimes caused by cancer. There are claims that a dog was able to detect his owner's breast cancer; another made news by sniffing out skin cancer.

Researchers are experimenting with bio-detection dogs in Japan, Germany, and other countries around the world. There is even talk that they may try to develop a mechanized nose that can replicate the accuracy of a dog's. Could that be possible? At this point it is tough for hospitals to embrace using actual dogs. After all, they are dogs.

Dogs shed. Dogs need to be walked. Dogs need attention. Will they be able to find a place in the sterile halls of your local hospital? We'll just have to wait and see.

This two-year-old beagle is making the rounds in a Holland hospital with his trainer Hotsche Luik and Dr. Marije Bomers. Cliff is trained to sniff out the dangerous *Clostridium difficile* (often shortened to *C. diff*) bacteria in patients, which can cause severe diarrhea and even death. After only two months on the job, Cliff can sniff out the superbug in a hospital ward in less than ten minutes just by walking around the beds of patients. This super sniffer is now making news all over Europe.

WAG MORE

Gatsby and I head out for our walk. He stops. Sniffs. I wonder what he smells. Who's been here before us? Or what? Was it the neighbor's cat or chickens? Was it one of those coyotes we heard howling last night? Or just the toad we see on warm nights? Maybe he smells one of those, or maybe all of them. I wish he could tell me.

So what's the difference between my dog, Gatsby, and the working sniffer dogs in this book? Training, of course. Gatsby is probably the only one who can get distracted by a squirrel. And although he loves a good hike, he's too much of a couch potato to work six to eight hours a day. Of course, I know he'd love to be with me 24/7, but then again, he pretty much is. He has the self-appointed job of guarding my office and keeping me company while I work. Most writers have a first reader. I have a first listener—Gatsby. He probably would love to meet all the dogs in this book, but in his own way he did. He sniffed each and every one upon my arrival home.

Shirley Hammond, longtime SAR-dog handler, told me that we are always learning from our dogs. And I believe her. The dogs I was privileged to meet during the writing of this book amazed me. They work hard. They play hard. They want to please, love, and share our lives more than we sometimes realize.

Is there no end to what they can do for us? And can we ever repay them?

ACKNOWLEDGMENTS

It would not have been possible to write this book without these amazing sniffer dogs. I cannot thank them enough for letting me tell their stories. The unique experiences I shared with them made writing this book a daily adventure. I couldn't have had more fun!

There was the endless game of fetch with Rocky in the mall parking lot. Exploring the catwalks and tunnels of Grand Central Terminal with Seren and Falcone. Watching Buford track his hider in just minutes, with bloodhound drool flying in the air and on me. Holding my breath as Raider worked "the pile." The light bulb moment I had as Ella zigzagged her way in and out of the scent cone as she searched the brush for her ball during a family barbecue. Witnessing Alan's alert in a high school gym. Standing in the snow watching Braith and Ashes scamper across charred wood to sniff out accelerants. Being "found" by Lex in a North Carolina forest. And the jaw-dropping moment Zuma alerted to a dime-size sprinkling of cremains.

I deeply appreciate the handlers who shared their dogs with me. They were so generous with their time and

Buford: southern Pride bloodhound on the job, search and rescue.

showed such great affection for their dogs. I hope I was able to capture their spirit and enthusiasm within these pages. My thanks go out to canine search specialist and trainer Shirley Hammond, Sara Rathbun of the Los Angeles Fire Department, Sgt. Ed O'Flaherty and Officer Greg Rozsay of the New York City MTA, Heath Smith of Conservation Canines, Alice Whitelaw and Aimee Hurt of Working

Cletus: a Southern Pride bloodhound super-sniffer.

Dogs for Conservation, Donna Randolph and Lynne Angeloro of the Institute for Canine Forensics, Officer Don Jones of the Guilderland Police, New York fire investigators Bill McGovern and John Fairclough, and Loki's handler, Donald Lysle.

I also want to thank Heidi Kretser of the Wildlife Conservation Society, Pat Phillips of the Pintler Pets Animal Shelter, Sherry Mers of Angel Service Dogs, Ron Aiello of the U.S. War Dogs Association, Cheryl Trefzgar of Warren Retrievers, Celeste Matesevac and Denise Hess of the Search Dog Foundation, Michelle Ninstat, Deputy Chief Randi Shadic, Vince Costello, Southern Pride Bloodhounds, Marije Bomers, Diane Whetsel, and Dave Vesely for their expertise, patience, and enthusiasm for this project.

I am thankful for the friends and writing buddies who supplied me with endless tidbits of doggie news that took me into new directions and explorations. Liza Frenette kept me in the loop about the AROMA project in the Adirondacks that inspired this book and another. I learned about the historic bone detectors from Lois and Paul Huey. Celeste Hosford first told me about the diabetes alert dogs and Barbara Wolff passed along the Dalmatian Days info that enabled me to photograph Cheyenne. My thanks to the Engel family, who graciously and enthusiastically allowed sniffer dogs onto the scene after their house fire for me to photograph.

My thanks also go out to my WOW ladies—Lois Huey, Liza Frenette, Kyra Teis, Helen Mesick, and Rose Kent—who constantly read my work and provide me with so much more than a monthly critique. I am ever grateful to them.

Gratitude and love to my husband, Dean, and daughter, Lucie, who continually offer their patience and enthusiasm, and in this case, even in the midst of dog drool. Love to them both!

Last, I extend many woofs and tail wags to my agent, Jennifer Laughran, and to my Houghton Mifflin Harcourt team, including the superdesigner Rachel Newborn, and my editor Erica Zappy, who shared her unending enthusiasm for dogs and encouraged mine.

BIBLIOGRAPHY

Ackerman, Diane. *A Natural History of the Senses*. New York: Random House, 1990.

American Rescue Dog Association. *Search and Rescue Dogs: Training the K-9 Hero*. New York: Howell Book House, 2002.

Angeloro, Lynne, historic human remains handler, Institute for Canine Forensics. Telephone interview. July 30, 2012.

Bauer, Nona Kilgore. *Dog Heroes of September 11th: A Tribute to America's Search and Rescue Dogs*. Allenhurst, N.J.: Kennel Club, 2006.

Bidner, Jen. *Dog Heroes: Saving Lives and Protecting America*. Guilford, Conn.: Lyons, 2002.

Boehm, David A. *Pictorial History of Fire Fighting: Going to Blazes*. New York: Castle, 1967.

Brennan, Heather. "Migaloo Is the World's First Archaeology Dog." *All Pet News*, January 31, 2013.

"CADA/Canine Accelerant Detection Association." September 28, 2012. cadafiredogs.com.

Catlin, George, and Peter Matthiessen. *North American Indians*. New York: Viking, 1989.

Charleson, Susannah. *Scent of the Missing: Love and Partnership with a Search-and-Rescue Dog*. Boston: Houghton Mifflin Harcourt, 2010.

Conservation Dog Programme Factsheet: Volunteer, Join or Start a Project Publication.
October 4, 2012. www.doc.govt.nz/publications/getting-involved
/volunteer-join-or-start-a-project/conservation-dog-programme
-fact-sheet.

Costello, Vince, rare snail conservation specialist, University of Hawaii. Email
interview. October 20, 2010.

Craven, B. A., E. G. Paterson, and G. S. Settles. "The Fluid Dynamics of
Canine Olfaction: Unique Nasal Airflow Patterns as an Explanation of
Macrosmia." *Journal of the Royal Society Interface* 7, no. 47 (2010): 933–43.

Derr, Mark. *How the Dog Became the Dog: From Wolves to Our Best Friends.* New
York: Overlook Duckworth, 2011.

Hammond, Shirley M. Telephone interview. October 5, 2012.

———. *Training the Disaster Search Dog.* Wenatchee, Wash.: Dogwise Publications, 2006.

Hepper, P. G. "The Discrimination of Human Odour by the Dog." *Perception* 17
(1988): 549–54.

Hepper, P. G., and D. L. Wells. "How Many Footsteps Do Dogs Need to Determine the Direction of an Odour Train?" *Chemical Senses* 30 (2005): 291–98.

Horowitz, Alexandra. *Inside of a Dog: What Dogs See, Smell, and Know.* New York:
Scribner, 2009.

"Industry Statistics & Trends." American Pet Products Association. n.d. Web.
January 14, 2013.

Johnson, Zack. Personal interviews. July 25, 2012; July 30, 2012; October 11, 2012.

Jones, Don, Guilderland Police. Personal interview. September 21, 2012.

Kretser, Heidi, AROMA Project, Wildlife Conservation Society. Personal interview. October 1, 2012.

Lowe, Esie L., and David E. Robinson. *Firehouse History, 1775–1975*. Village Mailer, Inc., Lunenburg, Mass., 1975.

M. M. "Dogs Help Save Endangered Species." *Dog Fancy*, August 2011, 14.

Mers, Sherry. Telephone interview. September 26, 2012.

National Association of Canine Scent Work. www.nacsw.net.

O'Flaherty, Ed, and Greg Rozsay, MTA K9 Unit. Personal interview. August 29, 2012.

Overton, Kayla. "A Dog 'Tail' of Two Snails." Official Homepage of the United States Army. March 29, 2010. www.army.mil/article/36531/A_dog_039_tail_039_of_two_snails.

Owen, Mark, and Kevin Maurer. *No Easy Day: The Autobiography of a Navy SEAL; The Firsthand Account of the Mission That Killed Osama Bin Laden*. New York: Dutton, 2012.

"Penn Vet Working Dog Center." October 3, 2012. pennvetwdc.org.

Phillips, Pat, Pintler Pets Animal Shelter. Telephone interview. October 16, 2012.

Pisano, Beverly. *Dalmatians*. Neptune City, N.J.: T.F.H. Publications, 1997.

"Puppies Behind Bars." www.puppiesbehindbars.com.

Randolph, Donna, historic human remains handler, Institute for Canine Forensics. Personal interview. October 20, 2012.

Rathbun, Sara, Los Angeles Fire Department, Search Dog Foundation. Personal interview. August 7, 2012.

Reitz, Stephanie. "Allergy-Sniffing Service Dogs Keep Kids Safe." Msnbc.com, June 9, 2011. www.msnbc.msn.com/id/43338485/ns/health-pet_health/t/allergy-sniffing-service-dogs-keep-kids-safe.

Schwartz, Marion. *A History of Dogs in the Early Americas*. New Haven: Yale University Press, 1997.

"Search Dog Foundation." June 2012. www.searchdogfoundation.org.

"September 11 Anniversary Rescue Dog Heroes." The Internet Home of Steve Dale. September 3, 2011. www.stevedalepetworld.com.

Shadic, Randi, New York State Fire Prevention and Control. Personal interview. September 7, 2012.

Smith, Heath, Conservation Canines. Telephone interview. July 19, 2012.

"Sniff, Serve, and Protect." *University of Pennsylvania Gazette* (2012): 46.

Southern Pride Bloodhounds of West Milford, N.J. Personal interview. September 22, 2012.

"SWGDOG Approved Guidelines." Scientific Working Group on Dog and Orthogonal detector Guidelines. September 23, 2012. www.swgdog.org.

Syrotuck, William G. *Scent and the Scenting Dog*. Rome, N.Y.: Arner Publications, 1972.

Thorwaldson, Jay. "'Disaster Dog' at Work in New York." *Palo Alto Weekly* (online edition), September 26, 2001. www.paloaltoonline.com/weekly /morgue/2001/2001_09_26.snifferside.html.

Trefzgar, Cheryl, Guardian Angel Retrievers/Warren Retrievers. Personal interview. July 6, 2012.

"Tsunami Impact on Pondicherry." MapsofIndia.com. January 9, 2013.

"Welcome." Arson Dog Training Program Sponsored by State Farm. Web. 2012.

"What Is the PETS Act?" ASPCA Professional: Disaster Preparedness. October 17, 2012. www.aspcapro.org/what-is-the-pets-act.php.

Whetsel, Diane, The Sage Foundation for Dogs. Telephone interview. April 1, 2013.

Whitelaw, Alice, Working Dogs for Conservation. Telephone interview. September 2010.

Wright, R. H. *The Sense of Smell*. Boca Raton, Fla.: CRC, 1982.

SUGGESTED READING

Bial, Raymond. *Rescuing Rover: Saving America's Dogs*. New York: Houghton Mifflin, 2011.

Charleson, Susannah. *Scent of the Missing: Love and Partnership with a Search-and-Rescue Dog*. Boston: Houghton Mifflin Harcourt, 2010.

Kroll, Virginia L., and Xiaojun Li. *Selvakumar Knew Better*. Fremont, Calif.: Shen's, 2006.

Paulsen, Gary, and Ruth Wright Paulsen. *My Life in Dog Years*. New York: Delacorte, 1998.

PLACES TO SNIFF OUT

Hartsdale Pet Cemetery: www.petcem.com.

New York State Museum: Visit the World Trade Center exhibit and see the tribute to the search dogs.

West Coast War Dog Memorial, Riverside, California: www.roadsideamerica.com/story/6600.

The Wild Center, Tupper Lake, New York: www.wildcenter.org. Visit the center and watch the film *Scent of the Moose* about Project AROMA.

See dogs at work at all international airports. Visit Grand Central Terminal in New York City to see the MTA K9s at work.

AND IF YOU ARE OVERSEAS

See the Hachiko statue outside the Shibuya Station in Tokyo.

See the Greyfriars Bobby statue in Edinburgh, Scotland.

See the Fido statue in Dante's Square in Borgo San Lorenzo, Italy.

WEBSITES

American Kennel Club Kids' Corner: A terrific online newsletter offering tips on dog ownership and activities.

www.akc.org/public_education/kids_corner/kidscorner.cfm

How to Love Your Dog: A Kid's Guide to Dog Care:

loveyourdog.com

Watch Zuma's early puppy detection training:

www.youtube.com/watch?v=DIPw7-Cpeig

Rusk family adoption ceremony of their son's military dog, Eli:

www.youtube.com/watch?v=EB0MqNOxtm0

Watch the Animal Planet show on the ICF dogs working in Bodie:

hhrdd.org/animalplanet.htm

It takes thousands of dollars to train one detection dog. Find out more about the organizations in this book and how you can support their efforts.

Conservation Canines/Conservation Biology, University of Washington

conservationbiology.net/conservation-canines

Institute for Canine Forensics

www.k9forensic.org

Search Dog Foundation

wwww.searchdogfoundation.org

Working Dogs for Conservation

workingdogsforconservation.org

WAYS TO GET INVOLVED

U.S. War Dogs: Military Working Dog Teams are always in need of items. Check out the U.S. War Dogs Association list of needed items and get together with your friends or scout troop to send some off to them!

www.uswardogs.org/needed-items

K9 Nose Work: You don't have to have a working scent dog to experience the thrill and fun of seeing your dog's nose in action. K9 Nose Work is an activity that gets pet dogs involved in scenting. The sport is sanctioned and organized by the National Association of Canine Scent Work. It runs workshops, classes, and competitions nationwide.

www.k9nosework.com/home.html

The Sage Foundation for Dogs Who Serve: Handlers with retired sniffer dogs can request aid in the form of free or discounted veterinary services. The foundation will also help place retired sniffer dogs. You can help by providing services, donations, or ideas to help these hero dogs.

www.sagefoundationfordogs.org

Search Dog Foundation: SDF has partnered rescued dogs with firefighters throughout the United States in an effort to provide trained search and rescue teams to be deployed in the event of disasters or other emergencies. You can help their efforts by sponsoring a search dog or volunteering.

www.searchdogfoundation.org/how_to_help

GLOSSARY

accelerant detection dog: a dog trained to detect the presence of ignitable liquids, including gasoline, jet fuel, paint remover, diesel fuel, and kerosene.

air-scent dog: a search dog that sniffs the air for the scent of a person or thing.

alert: a signal given to a handler upon a successful detection.

allergy alert dog: a dog trained to detect particles of certain foods, such as peanuts, shellfish, soy, and dairy, that cause severe allergies in certain people.

cadaver dog: a dog that searches for human remains.

canine: a dog. Derived from the family name Canidae.

cremains: the remains left after the process of cremation.

diabetes alert dog: a dog trained to detect the low and high blood sugar levels in individuals with type 1 diabetes.

disaster dog: a dog trained to search in collapsed buildings and other disaster situations.

eco dog: a dog trained to assist conservation scientists in the field.

FEMA: Federal Emergency Management Agency. FEMA is a U.S. government agency that responds to federal disasters.

historic human remains detection dog: a dog trained to search for buried bones.

human remains detection dog: a more appropriate name for a cadaver dog.

K9: homophone for "canine"; a dog specially trained to assist the police.

kill shelter: an animal shelter where animals deemed unadoptable are euthanized. Fortunately, many animal shelters have now adopted a no-kill policy, but kill shelters still exist.

lead: leash.

live-find dog: a dog trained to search for living people.

military working dog: a dog trained to assist the military in finding hostile humans and explosives. These dogs are also used as guards and sentries.

narcotics detection dog: a dog trained to detect marijuana, cocaine, heroin, and methamphetamines, among other drugs.

off-lead: off-leash; running free.

on-lead: held by a handler on a leash.

SAR: search and rescue.

scent cone: the cone that scent forms as it disperses in the air. The shape of the cone depends on wind and moisture.

tracking dog: a search dog that sniffs the ground for the scent of a person or thing.

working dog: a dog employed as a service dog or detection dog.

PHOTO CREDITS

INDEX

Page numbers in **bold** refer to photos.